Uncoverings 1980

Volume 1 of the Research Papers of the
American Quilt Study Group

edited by Sally Garoutte

Copyright © 1981 by the
American Quilt Study Group.
All rights reserved.

Copyright note: This is a collective work.
AQSG holds the copyright to this volume and
any reproduction of it in whole. Rights to individual
articles are held by the authors. Requests for
permission to quote or reproduce material from
any article should be addressed to the author.

Published by the American Quilt Study Group
660 Mission Street, Suite 400
San Francisco CA 94105-4007
Manufactured in the United States

Third printing 1993
ISBN 1-877859-03-6
ISSN 0227-0628
Library of Congress catalog card number: 81-649486

Cover photo: *Inscription* (1874–1876)
made by Cornelia Catharine Vosburgh,
of Red Hook, New York
Private Collection
Photo courtesy of Roderick Kiracofe

This volume is supported by a generous donation from
Winifred Sharp Reddall,
a founding member of American Quilt Study Group

Contents

Foreword 1

RESEARCH PAPERS

Barbara Brackman, *Midwestern Pattern Sources* 3
Lucille Hilty, *The Passion For Quiltmaking* 13
Sally Garoutte, *Early Colonial Quilts in a Bedding Context* 18
Joyce Gross, *Four Twentieth Century Quiltmakers* 28
Sandra Metzler-Smith, *Quilts in Pomo Culture* 41
Bets Ramsey, *Design Invention in Country Quilts of Tennessee and Georgia* 48
Winifred Reddall, *Pieced Lettering on Seven Quilts Dating from 1833 to 1891* 56

SPECIAL PRESENTATIONS

Cuesta Benberry, *Afro-American Women and Quilts: An Introductory Essay* 64
Jean T. Federico, *White Work Classification System* 68
John L. Oldani, *Archiving and the American Quilt: A Position Paper* 72

Foreword

These research papers and special presentations on aspects of the history of American quilt art were initially presented at the first meeting of the American Quilt Study Group in November 1980 in Mill Valley, California. They are now published with considerable pleasure by the Directors of AQSG.

The first Seminar was undertaken with some trepidation. We did not then know whether there was enough serious interest among American women in their own indigenous art to call forth the effort of research necessary to make up a program of papers. This book is the best sort of evidence that such interest indeed exists. It introduces the public audience as well as quilt lovers to the idea that the history of quilts and quiltmaking is an important part of our heritage, subject to serious study. The American Quilt Study Group hopes that this volume is the first of many.

My heart felt thanks go to the authors who have suffered through my first experience of editing. Theirs are the ideas, the work and the words; mine are any errors in transmission.

Sally Garoutte, editor

Midwestern Pattern Sources

Barbara Brackman

During the twentieth century the printed media - books and periodicals - has had a profound effect upon our lives and culture. Quiltmaking is no exception. From the turn of the century the printed media has definitely affected the way quilts look. In nearly any quilt display one comes across examples of 19th century quilts which appear to be one of a kind, with no printed source. These 19th century quilts are unique — either designs original to the maker or patterns passed on in families and communities in the folk tradition. But not so with 20th century quilts. Time and time again we find quilts made after 1900 which seem unique, but a little research points out that there is a published source for the design. An Art Deco fan from Holstein's THE PIECED QUILT seems to be a novel pattern, but a short search finds that it is one of the patterns syndicated by The Old Chelsea Station Needlecraft Company published in the 30's when this quilt was made. It is only the color arrangement of Holstein's example which makes it unusual. Again, a recent copy of THE QUILT ENGAGEMENT CALENDAR by Cyril Nelson featured a pattern about which he says, "the maker of this quilt translated her patriotism into a very effective design." A search turns up the fact that the maker translated a FARM JOURNAL pattern called Red, White and Blue from 1945 into her quilt.

I have had many similar experiences in which what looks to be a unique 20th century quilt turns out to be made from a published commercial pattern. I am now very skeptical when anyone tells me they have a one of a kind or original 20th century quilt. With a little digging I,

Barbara Brackman, MA, University of Kansas, has taught in high school, preschool and college. A quiltmaker since college years, her interest expanded to pattern collecting. Author and compiler of AN ENCYCLOPEDIA OF PIECED QUILTS, and many articles. Address: 500 Louisiana St., Lawrence, KS 66044.

or another pattern collector, can come up with a printed source. Of course recent trends in quiltmaking are producing many original 20th century quilts designed by quiltmaker/artists, so the time I am talking about is primarily 1920-1970. My experiences with these mid 20th century quilts have made me realize how pervasive the influence of the commercial sources have been.

I'd like to discuss two of these commercial sources as representatives of the development of media sources in pattern history. Both are midwestern; in fact, both are within 50 miles of my home in Kansas. The stories of CAPPER'S WEEKLY and Aunt Martha's Studios are typical of the midwestern pattern sources in the mid-twentieth century and typical of the effect they have had on pattern history and quilt design.

Being an incorrigible categorizer, I have decided there are two kinds of quilt patterns. Original patterns are those designed by a person who is identifiable, if not by name by some identity. These patterns are designed by talented amateur quiltmakers or salaried designers. The other type of pattern is the folk pattern. Of course a folk pattern had to have been designed by someone at some time, but the origins are lost; there is no identifiable designer. To go beyond the family or neighborhood in which it is passed on orally, the pattern must be "Found" and then published. Goose Tracks is a pattern which the Ladies' Art Company found and published in their catalog around the turn of the century. It is popular still, a pattern which was found and remained found.

Some patterns are passed on in folklore, found and published, and then lost again. I feel the work of serious pattern collectors is "refinding" patterns. Many of the folk patterns were originally found by writers or by reader contributors to small regional farm newspapers with small circulations — CAPPER'S WEEKLY is a good example. The newspapers were read, the pattern ordered or copied, and a few quilts made. But then the newspaper was thrown away, the name of the pattern forgotten as it was handed down in quilt form and the pattern was lost again. It is up to us to find them a second time.

CAPPER'S WEEKLY is typical in many ways of the farm periodical sources. It is atypical in that it is still in business, publishing bi-weekly from Topeka, Kansas. Not much else has changed; there are no computer word processors to flash type on a green screen; the employees still read page proofs as they have for many years. CAPPER'S is now written for the small town family; it is a digest of news with a human interest slant — an optimistic good news type of paper with a circulation of 1 and ½ million. Although CAPPER'S has a 101 year history, I have concentrated on the mid-twentieth century during the second quilt revival, to use Cuesta Benberry's description.

The farm papers generally had one page for children and one or two pages for women, with the rest of the paper devoted to agricultural news and advice. CAPPER'S women's page was called "In the Heart of the Home." The editor was supposedly Kate Marchbanks, although this has always been a pen name. On February 12, 1927, an "Old Time Quilt Block" appeared with a note from Kate saying that "since old time pieced or patchwork quilts have again stepped in the limelight, the paper had received requests for quilt block ideas." Therefore, they would publish a few from an "old, old quilt book of a great-grandmother friend of ours."

The origin of the column is quite typical in that the editor was apparently responding to reader demand of the later 20 s. I had always attributed the revival of interest in quilt making during the 30's to the Depression when everyone needed an inexpensive hobby and inexpensive blankets, but reading the farm periodicals points out that the reader demand became so insistent around 1927 that most of the magazines began publishing patterns at that time, three years before the Depression. Of course farmers were never too prosperous during the 20 s, but the impetus for the revival of interest in quilts was not poverty but a general interest in Americana and antiques much as we are going through today in the third quilt revival. The interest during the late 20 s in colonial and American heritage is reflected in the fact that the Williamsburg, Virginia restoration project was funded in 1926. Period furniture was also quite popular at that time.

Responding to this interest CAPPER'S WEEKLY began printing a few quilt patterns taken from the "old, old book" which was apparently The Ladies' Art Company Catalog, a popular source. The editor of "The Heart of the Home" page was actually Louise Fowler Roote. She apparently researched the column, although whether she drew it is unknown. The drawings began with a rather stolid Ladies' Art Co. style, but the column quickly developed into an original and well-drawn quilt pattern feature. Roote mentioned that she had a trunk full of old quilts which were her initial inspiration after the old booklet. Over the next 8 years Roote's Kate Marchbanks quilt column produced a regular, weekly collection of patterns from several sources:

1. She copied earlier sources, such as the Ladies' Art Co. catalog. This was common in many columns, but CAPPER'S seems to have resorted to it only occasionally.
2. She documented old quilts from the Topeka area. After using the

patterns from the quilts in her trunk, she began documenting other antique patterns which had previously been unpublished. The column featured quilts from museums, fairs and quilt shows as well as from private collections. Roote was, in essence, finding folk patterns.

3. She documented contemporary quilts, printing fair winners and other original designs.

4. She also printed some original designs which either she or staff artists designed specifically to be sold as patterns.

The drawings of these patterns appeared in the newspaper and readers could send in 15¢ to receive an actual pattern. Unfortunately I have none of the full-size patterns, neither does CAPPER'S, nor Mrs. Roote.

At the same time patterns were appearing in CAPPER'S WEEKLY, the Capper Publishing Company was also publishing other magazines such as HOUSEHOLD JOURNAL and the KANSAS FARMER AND MAIL AND BREEZE. The identical patterns found in CAPPER'S WEEKLY were also offered for sale in these periodicals. A few catalogs were also printed which offered the newspaper patterns for sale. As far as I know, there were no pamphlets offering full size patterns in the early years of the column.

In 1935 Capper's quilt column began to fade out, replaced by a syndicated quilt column. Apparently Mrs. Roote found it easier to run syndicated mail order patterns than to continue writing a column on her own. By buying a syndicated column she no longer had to search for quilts, draw the illustrations, draft the patterns and sell them by mail order. The syndicated column did all that for her. Unfortunately, the coming of the syndicated column meant the end of the regional newspaper as a regional source for local folk patterns. No longer was a Topeka paper finding and printing Topeka patterns. The syndicated column homogenized quilt making across the country. While the syndicated columns such as 'Home Art', 'Old Chelsea Station' or 'Aunt Martha' developed a new and extensive body of patterns, it is unfortunate that they supplanted so many original, regional sources like CAPPER'S.

After 1935, CAPPER'S began carrying a large number of syndicated columns including 'Old Chelsea Station', 'Aunt Martha', 'Home Art' and 'Famous Features'. In the 1950's Roote, who was by this time editor of the entire paper, and Mabel Obenchain, a writer for 'Famous Features', compiled some of the old Capper's patterns into a pamphlet called KATE'S BLUE RIBBON QUILTS. In the first printing of this booklet Roote wrote a foreword, but later editions eliminated the foreword and her credit. The booklet became BLUE RIBBON QUILTS. As Roote says today, "I am the forgotten woman." Capper's has sold Famous Features syndicated booklets since the 1950's. BLUE RIBBON QUILTS was followed by 17 others, some of which contain CAPPER'S patterns from Louise Roote's 'Heart of the Home' column. Many of the pamphlets are still in print and available in a number of periodicals.

The story of CAPPER'S WEEKLY illustrates how the syndicated column replaced the regional column in the mid 30's. The 'Aunt Martha/Workbasket' syndicate is typical of many such organizations. Generally the syndicated column featured a small drawing of a quilt pattern supplied by the pattern house in a newspaper or magazine. The reader who was enticed by the drawing would send 10 or 15¢ to the address listed, generally something like Quilt Pattern Dept., in care of the newspaper. All mail addressed to that department was actually forwarded to the syndicated pattern company who then sent the reader her pattern by mail. The 'Aunt Martha' syndicate followed this method of operation. It is typical in other ways. It is still in business, and its patterns were generally original patterns designed by professional artists rather than folk patterns as the majority of the patterns which appeared in the regional periodical columns were.

While the syndicates did some folk pattern dissemination, they made a significant change in pattern sources by hiring designers to develop original patterns. Some of the designers are well-known; Ruby McKim and Anne Orr are two whose patterns were signed, and two who owned their own companies — no coincidence. Most of the designers were anonymous. The use of professional artists was a significant change because it took quilt patterns from the class of a folk art to a commercial art. Some people feel this is a decline in the art. Whether or not it was a change for the worse, it was definitely a change.

The history of Aunt Martha's Studios is as complex as that of any Eastern European country, with name changes and different wings of the company. I will try to summarize the relevant facts. In the early 30's Jack and Clara Tillotson of Kansas City began the Colonial Readicut Quilt Block Co. as a response to the quilt revival at the time. They recently recalled for me that selling quilt kits was impractical because people could not afford them. The Tillotsons then switched to selling the patterns for the quilts for a dime. They shortened the name of the company to The Colonial Pattern Company.

The Tillotsons used the syndicated format to sell their patterns in the newspapers and magazines. The columns are usually under the name 'Aunt Martha'. That homey name derived from an incident in a Chicago newspaper in which the editor ran the column under the byline Martha Tillotson. (If you will recall, Mrs. Tillotson's name was Clara.) Mr. Tillotson guessed that the man chose the name Martha because it sounded colonial, Martha Washington being the best know Colonial dame. The Tillotsons were uncomfortable with the use of the family name and suggested the editor change the byline to Aunt Martha, which was both colonial and anonymous. Soon the name 'Aunt Martha' became better known than Colonial Pattern Company which was fortunate for pattern collectors since many other companies were also using the name Colonial at the time.

To add to our confusion the Tillotsons began another arm of the business when they added WORKBASKET magazine in the mid thirties. Aunt Martha's column generally consisted of a hodgepodge of patterns, a collection of needlework ideas. They began calling this collection The Workbasket and in 1935 began a formal magazine called AUNT MARTHA'S WORKBASKET. After a few issues the name was shortened to WORKBASKET and has continued until the present. WORKBASKET has always been primarily a source of other types of needlework pattern such as crochet and knitting patterns rather than exclusively quilt patterns. During the first few years at least one quilt pattern was included in every monthly issue and others were advertised as for sale from the Aunt Martha Studios. The full size patterns which appeared in WORKBASKET were also included in Aunt Martha's syndicated column. In fact at one point if one sent off for an 'Aunt Martha' pattern one received a WORKBASKET magazine. It seems hopeless to try to distinguish between WORKBASKET and 'Aunt Martha' patterns and collectors don't. Many of the patterns which are in the Aunt Martha pamphlets still in print were originally in WORKBASKET. Additional confusion occurs because these were not the only names used by the company. Later on the quilt patterns were sold through WORKBASKET under the name of 'Aunt Ellen' and I have seen one Aunt Martha column with a byline of 'Betsy Ross'. Furthermore, about 1940 the parent company became known as Modern Handcrafts.

If you are looking for quilt patterns in WORKBASKET, the best years are 1935-1940. During the war they appeared with less frequency as the quilt revival lost momentum. From 1945-1952 a few were printed and as far as I know none have been printed since 1952. The reasons for this are two. One is the lack of interest in quilts in the late 40 s and the other that the Tillotsons sold their pattern arm in 1949. Aunt Martha Studios/ Colonial Patterns were sold to Mr. & Mrs. Clifford Swenson with the rights to all the quilt patterns. WORKBASKET does not print quilt patterns to this day since they felt this would be unfair competition with Aunt Martha. Aunt Martha Studios were sold again in 1974 to Edward Price who still publishes the patterns in pamphlet form. After the Tillotsons sold Aunt Martha they continued to advertise Aunt Martha patterns in WORKBASKET until 1977 or so. The Tillotson family continues to publish WORKBASKET. John II and John III manage Modern Handcrafts Co. which publishes other magazines as well.

I asked the elder Tillotsons about the sources for the patterns which appeared under the Aunt Martha and WORKBASKET names. Mrs. Tillotson recalled that they originally printed older patterns after doing research in the library. Since there were very few sources for patterns in 1930 I assume she meant Finley, McKim and other writers who were finding folk patterns. Mrs. Tillotson also mentioned that she went to fairs and exhibits looking for patterns. This is the source for a 1933 pamphlet called THE QUILT FAIR COMES TO YOU in which patterns from quilts shown at the Chicago World's Fair and others were advertised. This booklet seems to be the first publication of the pattern we now call Cathedral Window. Here it was called The Daisy Quilt. Initially Aunt Martha Studios did some finding of folk patterns.

Aunt Martha also obtained patterns by holding quilt block contests. One booklet called PRIZE WINNING DESIGNS featured unusual blocks from women throughout the midwest. These early pamphlets are now out of print. They were a documentation of old and contemporary folk patterns. Shortly Aunt Martha Studios began hiring professional designers to draw up Aunt Martha originals. I talked to Marguerite Weaver who went to work for WORKBASKET around 1936. She had been a student of Eveline Foland's — a name familiar to collectors of KANSAS CITY STAR patterns. Mrs. Weaver says she designed many types of needlework patterns but her specialty was stamped embroidery patterns, many of which are still for sale by Aunt Martha and WORKBASKET. She did do many quilt patterns also, and she recalled that the designs were original with her. The philosophy behind designing original patterns rather than collecting folk patterns seems to have been that since they were selling these patterns they were concerned about copyright problems. So few people at the time gave a thought to copyright or plagiarism that Aunt Martha is to be commended. Mrs. Weaver says that she and the other artists were quite careful to use only original designs. If she was inspired by a quilt she had seen she made changes in the design to make it original.

Aunt Martha Studios over the years has published a number of pamphlets. Cuesta Benberry gave me a bibliography of 14 booklets. Originally these were catalogs from which one could order a single pattern although they included a few full-sized patterns. In the 40 s they began the series which is still for sale. They are self contained with 11-17 full size patterns in each of the 8 or 9 still in print.

I chose to look at these two pattern companies for several reasons. I wanted to see where patterns come from. I wanted to explore the influence of the midwest in quilt design. And I wanted to find some lost patterns. I was surprised to find how much I could find about CAPPER'S WEEKLY and Aunt Martha. I found complete bound sets of CAPPER'S and WORKBASKET. I found all the artists and editors alive and most willing, in fact, eager to talk.

I want to close with the suggestion that you as people who are interested in quilt history might take on a similar project, refinding lost patterns, either alone or a as a guild. Find a regional periodical which published near you. Search out the bound or microfilmed copies of old pattern columns. Talk to the people who documented local patterns. You might want to as a guild project reprint or redraw these columns. Of course copyright is a consideration but not an obstacle. The East Bay Heritage Quilter's Guild took on an similar project and did a real service by reprinting Alice Beyers' 1934 QUILTING book. If you are interested in such a project and don't know of a nearby source write and ask me. I'll be glad to give you some suggestions.

It is time we found all these lost patterns and did something about keeping them found.

A Capper's/Famous Features Bibliography

A. Pamphlets from Capper's Publishing
  Whittemore, Margaret and Florence Wells. QUILTING, A NEW, OLD ART. Capper Publication, Topeka, Kansas, no date, (1928, according to C.B.). This is a catalog of patterns which may be ordered from Capper's. They did not appear in the newspaper, and seem for the most part to be from the earlier sources.
  HOUSEHOLD'S QUILT BLOCK SERVICE. No date, ca. 1930. Another shorter catalog.

B. Pamphlets from Famous Features Syndicate
*#116 Blue Ribbon Quilts (originally Kate's Blue Ribbon Quilts) by Louise Fowler Roote and Mabel Obenchain.
 #101 Flower Quilts
 #102 Grandmother's Quilts (1959)
 #103 All Year (1959)
 #104 Crib Quilts
 #105 Covered Wagon Quilts (1959)
 #106 Bible Favorites
 #107 ABC Quilts
 #108 Centennial Quilts
 #109 Early American Quilts
 #110 Star Quilts
 #111 Round the World
 #112 One Piece Quilts
 #118 Grandmother's Flower Quilts by Virginia Mann
      Bicentennial Quilts by Obenchain and Lengel
*#124 White House Quilts by Obenchain and Vera Lengel
*#125 Rose Quilts by Obenchain and Dorothea Pursell
*#126 All Time Quilt Favorites (1979) by Mabel Obenchain
      Quilts on Parade by Virginia Mann

*are pamphlets which are still in print, containing full-size patterns, available from Famous Features Syndicate, Box 4958, Chicago, Illinois 60680. The patterns in these are, in the words of Ms. Obenchain, "original, others come under the heading public domain." Some of these patterns were originally in 'The Heart of the Home' column in CAPPER'S WEEKLY.

An Aunt Martha/WORKBASKET Bibliography

Barbara Brackman (with much help from Cuesta Benberry)

A New and Easy Way to Make a Quilt (ca. 1931)
Favorites Old and New (#5511) (ca. 1932)
Prize Winning Designs (#300) (ca. 1933)
The Quilt Fair Comes to You (#5514) (ca. 1933)
Star Designs (#9450) (ca. 1942)
*Quilt Designs - Old Favorites and New (#3175)
*Aunt Martha's Favorite Quilts (#3230)
*Quilts - Modern and Colonial (#3333) (1955)
*Easy Quilts (#3500) (1958)
*Quilt Lover's Delight (#3540) (1960)
*Quilts (#3614) (1963)
*Bold and Beautiful Quilts (#3778)
*Patchwork Simplicity (#3779)
*Quilts - Heirlooms of Tomorrow (#3788)

*are pamphlets with full size patterns which are currently available from Colonial Patterns, Inc. 1441 Atlantic, Kansas City, MO 64116.

Others are out of print.

WORKBASKET magazine has published continuously since October, 1935.

A Passion for Quiltmaking

Lucille Hilty

My title comes from a question I raised in Pat Ferrero's film, QUILTS IN WOMEN'S LIVES. In the film I wondered why there is so much emotion invested in quiltmaking? Why do people feel so passionate about this craft? This intense interest that I feel about quiltmaking has also been expressed by other quiltmakers. How can the making of bed covers arouse such zeal, such passion and intensity? What is there about quiltmaking that is so all-encompassing?

I have been trying to find answers. I have examined my experiences and I have talked to other quiltmakers. I shall try to articulate reasons why I think quiltmaking evokes these kinds of feelings.

When I reached the age of 50 a shocking thought occurred to me. Now that I was half a century old, I would need to start to think about retirement! My first thoughts were not thoughts at all, but a panic reaction to the idea of future change.

I had been very actively involved in teaching young children. Teaching Kindergarten had required much energy and devotion, but I was challenged and content in my work. Life stretched out ahead of me with a seemingly endless parade of more, and yet more five year old children and their accompanying problems and challenges — that is, until I hit that 50 year old mark. I pushed the idea of retirement into my subconscious, and went back to teaching — this time to the then new experimental program of Follow Through. Occasionally the idea of retirement would peek out into my conscious thought, and firmly I would bury it again.

About this time I made a commitment to a friend who greatly admired my quilts. At Christmas I told her that I would help her make a

---

Lucille Hilty, MA, Columbia University, is a quilting designer and consultant. She taught kindergarten for many years in Japan, the United Kingdom and California. Her specialty is fine quilting. Address: 134 York Ave., Berkeley, CA 94708.

quilt the following year. My mother, with whom I had learned to quilt, had recently died, and I had brought all of her quilting equipment from Ohio to California. In helping my friend, I also revived my interest in quilt making. While I refreshed my recollections of how to go about making a quilt, we worked together on her project. My friend turned out to be an apt pupil and became an excellent quilter. We finished her quilt just about the time the quilt revival of the past decade began. I had the feeling that that quilt revival was meant just for me. I reveled in all of the new books that came out. I especially loved the historical books with the colored plates of beautiful quilts. With another friend we went searching through the new quilt stores to fine the "right" quilt for my friend to take to Great Britain as a special gift.

About that time that little thought about retirement pushed its way out of my subconscious again. This time I embraced the idea of retiring. I knew that I could spend the rest of my life making quilts. From that time on I looked forward to the time when my life would be free from school routines, bells and schedules. I have been retired for more than two years now, my life is filled with quilts and quilt making, and I have never been more content.

In 1977, I impulsively decided to attend the Lincoln Quilt Symposium. By that time I realized that I had developed a passion for making quilts, but because I mostly worked alone, I did not know how other quiltmakers were feeling about their craft. Walking into the auditorium, that first day of the symposium, I suddenly became aware that here were 500 women who felt as I did about making quilts. I felt a wonderful sense of community. I left the symposium greatly enriched by the knowledge that this craft, which had become all consuming to me was shared by many others and that it was a valid form of expression and creativity.

Just recently another experience indicated to me how widespread is this passion people feel for quiltmaking. Marilyn Davis, owner of the fabric store, Patience Corners in Albany, California, recently conducted a survey of quilters. The last question on the survey dealt with the affective part of quilting, and asked the quilter to express, if possible, what quiltmaking meant to her. I am indebted to Marilyn for sharing this part of the survey with me. Most of those who filled out the survey made an effort to respond to this question. The responses were poignant and touching.

Most quilters, above all, believed their quiltmaking to be a creative expression of their ideas. They talked about the tactile pleasure they had in working with fabrics. Some talked about the therapeutic quality of

A PASSION FOR QUILTMAKING 15

the act of quilting, its calming and restful effect. For one, it relieved her depression; for others, it opened doors to friendships especially with women of different ages. Some women found supportiveness among other women and identified with the women's movement through their quilting. Another important area was the linkage with the past, with their ancestors, or with women who have gone before, and a link with their children and friends now.

I should like to share with you what one woman eloquently wrote. She seemed to sum up what all of the others were saying.

Quiltmaking is the emotional center of my life. The planning is my most creative outlet and the piecing and quilting my meditation. I make quilts as an act of love for my friends and family. Each quilt is a story (abstract) which tells of feelings and ideas. My quilts are a journal.

Quiltmaking is a process, both trivial and profound. There are certain tasks (marking) which seem tedious and others, equally as routine and demanding precision (piecing) which seem glorious. Choosing fabrics is exhilerating and frustrating. There is in the process, in its life, which is at least a year for a bed-sized piece, the evolution of a relationship with the work.

I feel related to the women who made the quilts shown in the books I pore over. I study their work and see into their most intimate moments.

I am also a participant in the quilts my friends make. I share the joy and sorrow I know is captured in their work. Quiltmaking ties me to my most beloved grandmother. I have slept under the quilt she made for me since I was sixteen. When I began to make quilts I felt as if a central part of me had come home.

Quilts are humble and magnificent. They are bed covers for warmth and decoration for the most private room.

I rapture on. As is apparent quiltmaking is a rich, magic craft, akin, I think, to the making of boats and tools and furniture. Quilts are practical, especially when made from scraps, and useful and beautiful. They are made by hand over a long stretch of time. They *emerge* from piece to piece, block to block, section to section. The pieced top emerges again when quilted and again as it ages and fades and softens with use. The process is, from the first notion of color and design through to the end of its life, an unfolding story.

Obviously, others feel a great passion for quiltmaking, too. I have some subjective, personal opinions about the questions I first posed concerning the passion and emotion in quiltmaking.

First and foremost, quilting is a folk art and a craft. As such, its first requirement is that one who would make quilts must learn the craft —all of it, not just some portion of the craft. Once learned, the practitioner is free to explore creatively within the limits set by function and the materials used. The use and size of a quilt determine its shape and dimensions. The fabric and tools determine what can be done with it.

Women of the past acquired these skills early in life. Sewing was a necessity, and the women in a family had the responsibility for clothing the family and providing the bed covers and other necessary textiles. Sometimes these were processed in the home from the original fiber source, including spinning, weaving and sewing. Girls learned to sew at a very early age, and quiltmaking skills were learned along with garment making. Quiltmaking became an outlet for creative ideas, in part because women were systematically excluded from serious formal art education.

Today sewing skills are often harder for modern women to acquire. Several generations of women have not had to sew, and chose not to. Those who choose to sew today often come to it at a much later age, and have no sewing models in the home. Still, many women are learning to do fine stitching of various kinds, and are doing it very well. Women are coming to needlework by choice, because they find values and means of self-expression, as well as utility, in sewing. Our young quiltmakers want to make all the quilt, not just part of it. Many are rejecting the statement that Rose Kretzinger wrote in her book, THE ROMANCE OF THE PATCHWORK QUILT IN AMERICA, "When you have finished your "top" turn it over to an experienced quilter, for a beautiful quilt may be made or marred by the quilting." Many quiltmakers want to do all of the work on their quilts.

There is room for less than perfect quilting when one is learning a craft. It says something about the integrity of the quilter when she insists upon having a part in all of the processes. I personally feel that a person loses credibility as a quilter if she does not perform all of the steps in making a quilt.

As one goes through the various stages of making a quilt, there is a relationship that evolves between the maker and the quilt. When the quiltmaker misses one of the phases of quiltmaking one loses the tactile and textural experiences that are an integral part of quiltmaking.

I would like to see credit given to those skilled quilters who quilt other people's quilt tops, and I would like to believe that in our time the "anonymous" quilter will disappear.

As a folk art quilting relates intimately to people's lives and their culture. The passion and emotion come from the intertwining of the life experiences of the maker and those with whom the quilt has intimate contact. All of the painstaking work is worthwhile when this made object, the quilt, conveys a message of caring to someone dear. The quiltmaker reveals herself when she makes choices and decisions about pattern, fabric, color, texture and workmanship, and makes a strong statement about herself. That many women have found a means of defining their identity within this folk art form, whether the quilt is signed or not, is an emotion laden thought.

Ours is a wordy, verbose society. We try to articulate all of our experiences and ideas with language. But there remains a need to express some ideas in an intuitive, non-verbal form. Writing this paper, for example, is almost counterproductive, for I am trying to convey, with words, my feelings about making quilts. In so doing, I lose some of the essence of quiltmaking.

Making a quilt is an organic process, closely related to the deepest feelings one has about life and the society in which one lives, and those individuals with whom one is most intimate. As one progresses with the craft and one's skills improve, I believe the quiltmaker comes closer to the core of what her life and beliefs are all about. It is the union of the hands with the mind and the spirit. One's identity as a person becomes clarified and belief and practice and craft become a celebration of that life.

Early Colonial Quilts in a Bedding Context

Sally Garoutte

In an effort to illuminate the history of quilts in America, some early writers unfortunately did just the opposite. Using the writing style of fifty years ago, most historians did not document their sources, and simply stated their theories and surmises as though they were fact. Quilt historians were not different, and their theories, later quoted and referred to over and over, have almost obscured the real history of quilts. We have mostly been reluctant to challenge these theories directly because we honor the women who made them, and so now they occupy a solid position in the lore of quilts.

Folklore, however, is not history. Although we need the lore to understand what people thought and how they felt about things, we need history too. We need to know what happened and what people did, and we need to document it dependably. Part of seeking out the real history of women's work and art is clearing up some of the misconceptions that have been repeated so often. Like George Washington's cherry tree story, "it ain't necessarily so."

It is the purpose of this paper to examine two particular stories often included in the "history" of quilts. One is that the first American quilts were made from economic need, the need for warm bedding being so great that early colonial women pieced together all their fabric scraps to make quilts.[1] Another story is that quilts were common and ordinary bed furnishings in all colonial households.[2]

The questions posed here, then, are: to what extent did early colonial households contain quilts, and what were they like?

It is important to be clear about the time period being discussed. Although we often speak vaguely of a "colonial era", as though nothing changed in more than a century and a half, the colonial period was in

---

Sally Garoutte, BA, Goddard College, is a textile historian and writer who has published in QUILTER'S NEWSLETTER and QUILTERS' JOURNAL. Address: 105 Molino Ave., Mill Valley, CA 94941.

fact a time of accelerating change. It seems appropriate to me to divide the 1620-1780 colonial period into an early colonial period (17th century) and a late colonial period (18th century). This distinction, though still rather crude, allows consideration of early American quilts to take place in some more reasonable progression of time/history.

Definitions

It is also important to make distinctions between "quilts", "patchwork quilts", and "pieced quilts". The definitions I will use here are the definitions used in the 18th century. *Quilt* — the word by itself — means a bed quilt of whole cloth, quilted. *Patchwork* originally meant what we now more often call applique — the putting on of patches of cloth. It did not mean pieces of cloth seamed together. *Piecework* means: cloth specially cut to fit together when seamed, so that it finally makes a full-sized top. In the early colonial times — in the 17th century — there was no patchwork or piecework. There probably was not any patchwork or piecework on bedcoverings before 1750. That was also the opinion of Florence Peto, who had excellent access to very old quilts.[3] Therefore, the quilts discussed here are whole-cloth quilts.

Early quilts were definitely bedding, and to find them and find their place in 17th century life, it is necessary to look at the entire bedding context in which they existed. The bedding of the 17th century consisted primarily of woolen blankets, woolen bed ruggs, and coverlets — which were sometimes woolen and sometimes linen. In the 17th century, quilts were actually quite a rare item, so the major bedding items will be examined first.

Bed ruggs

In the 17th century, rugs were always for sleeping under. The word "rugg" comes from Scandinavia where it always meant a sleeping rug. The idea of putting textiles on the floor and walking on them is quite recent in Western history.

Ruggs were of a coarse woolen weave. The yarns were coarse and rather harsh. The poorer parts of the English wool clip were reserved for use in bed ruggs. Ruggs often — perhaps always — had a shag woven in. Samuel Johnson's dictionary of 1755 called them "coarse nappy coverlets used for mean beds." Several authorities think that the shag was always a knotted shag — and there is some evidence for this from some 18th century ruggs. No presently known 17th century ruggs are in existence. These were not the later embroidered ruggs. The early ruggs were made in England, and the shag was made in the loom — not applied later with a needle.

An early commentary on 17th century ruggs is in a letter written in 1634 by John Winter, manager of a fishing station on the coast of Maine, to Robert Trelawny, his employer and supplier in Plymouth, England. Winter reported:

"I bought some coats and ruggs last year after Captain Smart arrived into the country, hoping to have put them away to the Indians last winter, but could not. But have now put away the ruggs, but at the same price I bought them here. There is such a store of these goods brought here by the Barnstaple ships that all the traders are filled with them."

Among the long list of things he asked for, Winter included "2 dozen of Barnstaple ruggs, woven without seam. . . . but I pray," he wrote, "send no more hatts nor coverletts. The coverletts are not for this country. They will not pass to the English nor to the Indians, for they must have them soft and warm."[4]

Another reference can be found in Bradford's history OF PLYMOUTH PLANTATION. In 1631, Isaac Allerton who had come on the Mayflower, returned to England for a load of supplies. But all he brought back for Plymouth was 100 Barnstaple ruggs. He had rented out the rest of the ship's cargo space for freight headed for Boston. To make matters worse, Plymouth somehow got charged twice for the ruggs. Governor Bradford was still hot about it twenty years later when he wrote his history.[5]

The most reliable documentation of early household furnishing is found in legal documents of the day, primarily household inventories and wills. The evidence of legal records from four colonies will be examined later in this paper. These documents vary considerably in completeness of description. Most are not descriptive at all. However, according to early inventories, ruggs came in many colors - white, blue, green, red and yellow being mentioned. Occasionally they were "striped" or "speckled", but none were described as having any kind of woven figure or design. These plentiful ruggs from England were not like the embroidered ruggs made by American women in the following century.

Blankets

Early blankets are also non-existent. Records, however, show that they were truly the commonest type of bedding all through the colonial centuries and after. They are listed over and over in wills and inventories

QUILTS IN A BEDDING CONTEXT 21

— in many different kinds and colors. They were imported in large numbers for trading to Indians.

Even though Americans began making blankets very early, English blankets were generally of a better quality and continued to be brought over in remarkable quantities. They were traded all over the continent, and the trade has never stopped. The famous Hudson's Bay blankets are still made in England for sale in North America.

Blankets were much finer and softer than ruggs. They were made of softer wool, fulled and teased to produce a fine, fluffy nap. Blankets were sold as finished blankets — usually in pairs — and also as "blanketting" — that is, the whole piece as it came from the loom, large enough for 16 to 18 full width blankets. The best of these were Witney blankets made mainly in Witney, Oxfordshire, but also in Somerset and Devon. They were white or nearly white, and very soft, and up to 12 quarters in width. (A "quarter" meant a quarter of a yard. 12 quarters was equivalent to 3 yards.) This was English manufacture at its finest. In Benjamin West's famous painting of Penn's Treaty with the Indians, he painted the central event of presenting an Indian chief with a roll of this supple white woolen cloth. However, Indians liked blue better than white, and blue blankets became the standard trade item — with a few red and green ones at various occasions.

In the early colonial period, there is no record of blankets having been decorated except (often) with stripes at the ends. The stripes served the practical purpose of indicating where the piece of blanketting should be cut into individual blankets. In the second half of the 18th century, however, blankets were frequently decorated at the corners with embroidered crowns or with non-floral "rose" motifs which have a resemblance to a compass rose.

Coverlets

The third kind of bedding to be found in quantity in old records is coverlets. It is less clear what a coverlet was in the 17th century, as any bedcovering might be called a coverlet at some time. However, inventories listed blankets, ruggs, and coverlets separately, so they were neither blankets nor ruggs. Some inventories listed "coverlet yarn" also, but didn't specify whether it was woolen or linen. Some mentioned that they were "wrought" or "worked", meaning embroidered, but most did not. John Winter's letter of 1634 said he didn't want any more coverlets — they weren't soft and warm enough. Probably there was quite a variety of things that might be called coverlets. Possibly what distinguishes them from blankets and ruggs is that coverlets were mainly decorative rather than mainly warm.

Many coverlets remain from the late colonial period, and they are highly decorative. Some of these are linen, but an equal number are woolen. The woolen coverlets are frequently catalogued as "blankets", but the elaborate embroidery and (often) fringe mark them as intended for the top cover of the bed.

Quilts

Quilts in the early colonial period were few and far between. They were the most expensive bedding item inventoried. They were found in the households of well-to-do people, usually merchant-importers. They were almost certainly imported rather than home-made. In wills, a few were described: "my silken quilt", "cradle quilt, silk on one side and calico on the other," a "calico quilt" and a "blue quilted coverlet." The last three of these were actually in early 18th century wills. So few quilts were recorded in the 17th century, it is difficult to get even a sense of them. There are no references at all during early colonial period to pieced work or patchwork, however, for the good reason that those techniques were not yet practiced. Like the quilted petticoats of the period, bed quilts were quilted designs on whole cloth.

Documentation

The records consulted in this study are: the probate inventories of Providence, RI, from 1670 to 1726[6], the probate inventories of Plymouth colony from 1631 to 1687[7], the wills of New Hampshire from 1659 to 1717[8], and the wills and a few inventories of the Hartford district of Connecticut from 1640 to 1749[9]. Although the time periods of these four record groups do not neatly coincide, they are in each case the earliest records available. In considering that three of the record groups extend beyond the 17th century, I considered also the usual longevity of bedding and concluded that most of the bedding in the later inventories was probably 17th century bedding. Although this slightly begs the question of sticking to the 17th century data, it has the advantage of enlarging the data base. In fact, strictly within the 17th century records, only three quilts were to be found!

I have seen only a random selection of inventories from Virginia printed in historical magazines and mostly from prominent families. Although similar to New England inventories, I have not seen enough southern inventories to make any comment on southern colony bedding.

Inventories vary in completeness but are usually far more complete than wills. They also usually include the monetary values of things. Wills, on the other hand, have the advantage of showing which things were important to the legator. And they were sometimes more descriptive — especially women's wills.

Statistics

From the inventories of Providence and Plymouth, I have calculated the separate average values of the blankets, ruggs, coverlets and quilts, so it is possible to determine what their comparative values were to the people of the 17th and early 18th centuries.

In Providence, the average value of a blanket during the period examined was ten shillings. The average value of a rugg was 15-1/3 shillings, and of a coverlet 17 shillings. The average value of the five quilts recorded in Providence was 52 shillings.

The inventories of Plymouth show a remarkable similarity. There, a blanket was worth on average ten shillings, ruggs were worth an average of 15-1/3 shillings, but coverlets were worth only 11 shillings. The only quilt recorded in Plymouth in that period was in an inventory of 1633 —clearly an English quilt — and no separate value was assigned to it.

The wills of Connecticut and New Hampshire of course did not list monetary values.

Using the wills and inventories both, I have counted the number of blankets, ruggs, coverlets and quilts recorded. Many of the documents listed undifferentiated "bedding", and those were excluded from the calculations. The blanket totals are probably undercounted, as it was not unusual to find "blankets" listed with no number given. In those instances, I used the smallest possible plural number: two.

The Providence inventories list 239 blankets, 30 ruggs, 88 coverlets, and 5 quilts. The New Hampshire wills mention 36 blankets, 20 ruggs, 5 coverlets, and 2 quilts. In the Hartford wills 91 blankets, 23 ruggs, 27 coverlets and 2 quilts were specifically mentioned. In Plymouth there were inventoried 185 blankets, 85 ruggs, 39 coverlets and 1 quilt.

It is notable that Plymouth Colony records show such a large number of bed ruggs. Possibly it is a legacy of Isaac Allerton's poor business judgement in 1631.

The totals of these bedding items show 551 blankets, 158 ruggs, 159 coverlets, and 10 quilts. Adding these figures gives a total of 858 bedding items, of which only ten are quilts. This is only 1.16%.

Other studies

Two earlier studies of colonial household inventories in New England

NAMED BEDDING FOUND IN THE EARLY RECORDS OF PLYMOUTH, PROVIDENCE, HARTFORD AND NEW HAMPSHIRE

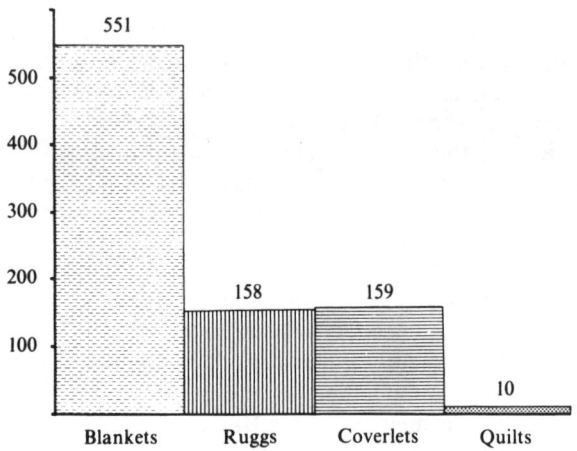

A. TOTAL NUMBER

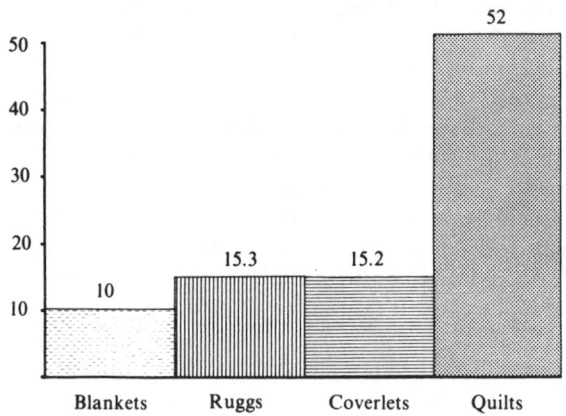

B. AVERAGE VALUE IN SHILLINGS

Graphics: Bill Garoutte

are of Essex County and Suffolk County, Massachusetts. More than fifty years ago George Francis Dow surveyed the Essex County (Salem area) inventories recorded between 1635 and 1674. In an article, Dow commented on his survey: "coverlets are mentioned 142 times and ruggs 157 times while quilts are listed only four times."[10] His article does not mention blankets.

In a study of fabrics used in interior furnishing, Linda R. Baumgarten examined 485 selected household inventories of Suffolk County (Boston area) between 1650 and 1695. In her paper published in the Winterthur Conference Report for 1974, Baumgarten stated: "Few quilts are listed in the inventories; the ones mentioned are described as calico, painted calico, and East India, indicating an Indian origin. Other quilts were silk. No references to pieced quilts were found."[11]

Thus the Salem and Boston areas provide the same picture as the four areas examined in this paper.

Conclusions

From this information, I have concluded that quilts were not common or ordinary articles in early colonial times. Far from it. They were both rare and expensive.

I have concluded also that quilts were not born of economic necessity or, at least primarily, as a practical means of keeping warm. There was clearly plenty of other, cheaper, bedding available — from domestic looms as well as English looms. Further, a significant number of late 18th century American quilts are not warm at all, containing as they do only the minimum amount of filling to show off the quilting. The "need" for American women to make handsome quilts does not appear to be either economic or practical.

Quilts in Early Colonial New England

1633		Plymouth. Samuel Fuller inventory. On flock bed.
1647	*	Salem. William Clarke inventory. 1 quilt on flock bed in chamber over kitchen.
1648	*	Ipswich. John Whittingham inventory. 2 quilts.
1685	*	Salem. George Corwin, merchant, inventory. In house,"1 large white quilt, 40s; 1 ditto, 30s; 1 ditto, 20s. 1 quilt of calico Colered & flowred, 30s."
1689		Portsmouth. Jane Joce, widow & merchant, will. "my silken quilt . ."
1693		Portsmouth. Joshua Moody, will. "one of the best quilts."
1712		Providence. Freelove Crawford, widow & merchant, inventory. 1 Calico bed quilt, 45s.
1720		Providence. William Whiteway, mariner, inventory. A quilt and a blanket, 35s.
1720		Providence. William Crawford, merchant, inventory. (Son of Freelove Crawford) 2 quilts, value not stated.
1721		Providence. John Jenckes, physician & merchant, inventory. a quilt, 60s.
1744		Hartford. Dorothy Stevens, will. "a cradle quilt, silk on one side calico on the other."
1748		Hartford. Mary Sweeny, will. "a blue quilted coverlid."

*Listed by George Francis Dow

References:
1. Ruth E. Finley, OLD PATCHWORK QUILTS, Branford, Newton Center, MA, 1970. (reprint of 1929 edition) p. 33.
2. Marie D. Webster, QUILTS: THEIR STORY AND HOW TO MAKE THEM, Doubleday, NY, 1915. p. 60.
3. Florence Peto, "New York Quilts", in NEW YORK HISTORY, vol. 30, no. 3, July 1949.
4. James Phinney Baxter, ed., The Trelawny Papers, DOCUMENTARY HISTORY OF THE STATE OF MAINE, vol. 3, Portland, 1884. pp. 25, 28, 45.
5. Samuel Eliot Morison, ed., William Bradford, OF PLYMOUTH PLANTATION, 1620-1647, Knopf, NY, 1952. pp. 227, 243.
6. Record Commissioners of Providence, THE EARLY RECORDS OF THE TOWN OF PROVIDENCE, vols. 6, 7, 1894. vol. 16, 1906.
7. Charles Henry Pope, ed., THE PLYMOUTH SCRAP BOOK, Boston, 1918; and THE MAYFLOWER DESCENDANT, vol. 1, 1889, vol. 2, 1900, vol. 3, 1901.
8. State Papers Series, vol. 31, Albert Stillman Batchellor, ed., PROBATE RECORDS OF THE PROVINCE OF NEW HAMPSHIRE, vol. 1 1635-1717, Concord, 1907.
9. Charles William Manwaring, ed., A DIGEST OF THE EARLY CONNECTICUT PROBATE RECORDS, Hartford District, vols. 1, 2, 1904. vol. 3, 1906.
10. George Francis Dow, "The Patchwork Quilt and Some Other Quilts," OLD TIME NEW ENGLAND, vol. 17, no. 4, April, 1927.
11. Linda R. Baumgarten, "The Textile Trade in Boston, 1650-1700," in ARTS OF THE ANGLO-AMERICAN COMMUNITY IN THE SEVENTEENTH CENTURY, ed. Ian M. G. Quimby, University Press of Virginia, Charlottesville, for Winterthur Museum, 1975. p. 233.

Four Twentieth Century Quiltmakers

Joyce R. Gross

Although a number of the nation's art museums have quilts in their collections made by nationally known quiltmakers, information about the quiltmakers has been almost totally lacking. In some instances, not even the significant dates of the artists were known by the museums. This I found to be highly frustrating, and so began research of my own into the lives of twentieth century quiltmakers.

Four of these master quiltmakers are presented here. Better known than many of their colleagues because their work is in museums and has been photographed for catalogs and other publications, they are not the only master quiltmakers of their period. The names of most quiltmakers still remain unknown to us.

Material for these biographies comes from diaries, letters, newspaper articles, and interviews with families and friends.

Myrtle Mae Fortner

Myrtle Mae Fortner is known for a single quilt, The Matterhorn, in the collections of the Denver Museum of Art. It has been shown in major exhibitions in Denver, at the Hallmark Gallery in New York, in the American Pavilion at Expo '70 in Osaka, Japan, and in San Francisco at two "Patch in Time" quilt shows and at the Bank of America Headquarters Gallery.

Born Myrtle Mae Melvin in Camden, Illinois, December 13, 1880, the artist was the ninth of ten children. When Mertie (as she was called by her family) was small, her older sister died leaving two daughters. Those two little girls, Flora and Myrtle, came to live with the Melvin family,

---

Joyce Gross, BA, University of California, is editor and publisher of QUILTERS' JOURNAL. She has organized and curated five major quilt shows, and is expert on quiltmakers of the 20th century and Hawaiian quilts. Address: P.O. Box 270, Mill Valley, CA 94942.

and Flora was to become a favorite of her aunt's. In the diary she kept in 1955, her 75th year, Mertie wrote: "This is Flora's birthday. I did not send her a card or a gift but insisted on paying for our lunch when we were in Lancaster on Saturday. No one can ever know how very much I have loved that precious baby. I myself was still playing with dolls when she was brought to our home at 2½ months. This one was far more loveable and interesting than any doll. I hope I have never failed her when I could be of help to her."

Mertie married her first cousin, Linneous Fortner, despite parental objection. Two years later she left, alone, for Los Angeles. On October 22, 1955, she wrote in her diary, "I was married in Denver, Colo. 54 years ago today. It doesn't seem that it can be so long ago. There is neither pleasure nor regret in the memory. It now seems that it was just an experience which was part of my education and no one was to blame - just two people with ideas and ideals so different that there could be no adjustment and I am glad it happened so soon."

In Los Angeles she became successful, building and managing apartment houses. During the depression she lost everything and was forced to start a new life in the small desert town of Llano, CA. With her own hands she built a small cabin. She had neither running water nor electricity but she managed a pleasant life. On August 14, she wrote, "I am glad to be left to my own quiet way except when some of my real friends or relatives come." On December 13, "I have spent the day alone but not lonely." Her life was made up of many everyday tasks. On January 22, she wrote, "Emptied ashes this A.M. That is a major operation . . . always three buckets full and a mess on the floor to be cleaned up. Melted some more snow. Carried in several loads of wood." February 1 she noted, "Cold & windy today. I have carried in 6 loads of wood and two of water. Looks like another storm in a day or two." On February 5 she wrote, "Just a quiet morning washing dishes. Hoped the man would be here to adjust the gas but he did not come." On August 16, she wrote, "Went to the store this afternoon and now have more variety to eat."

"Mertie" loved Scrabble games, which she played by herself and with her niece Flora who was a frequent visitor. On January 30 the diary reads, "I read aloud awhile this evening and then she beat me at Scrabble. I am sure I don't know why I never win games of any kind but that seems to be the case - Well I enjoyed the game - and we'll try it again. We always learn a few new words, but I wish they were longer ones instead of 3 to 5 letters as most of them are."

On March 29 she wrote, "Played a game of Scrabble this evening with

R & L representing 2 players - R won as usual though I favor neither -that one usually has letters that fit better." On Sunday May 15 she notes, "I played a solo game of Scrabble this evening and for the first time I got all of my 7 letters moved to the board at one time. The word was 'smeared' so I got 50 points for that but my score was still only 576. John May says his highest score was 665 out of a possible 1,000 so I'm not satisfied yet."

Quiltmaking is not mentioned in this diary but several references are made to the Matterhorn and a large braided rug which she had made. The first reference was on January 2, "This has been a good day. Four people came to see my quilt and braided rug. The quilt pieced in small squares - 9,135 of them and is a picture of the Matterhorn — mountains, stream, trees and rocks all in place — with two cabins." Her family believe that the two cabins represent her own and one belonging to Flora that she could see from her window. On June 5, she wrote, "They admired my quilt and rug."

Myrtle frequently mentioned her Christian Science faith and apparently read her lesson and the CHRISTIAN SCIENCE MONITOR faithfully.

Toward the end of the year 1955 Mrs. Fortner begins to mention that a change in her lifestyle will occur. On Sunday October 2, she noted, "We attended church at Victorville today. Went to the Desert Inn for lunch, bought the Sunday Times (from Los Angeles) and read it while listening to soft music being broadcast from the station in the morning. Had dinner here and have been looking at house plans again. I guess it is decided that I will put the house on the market and have a cottage built near Victorville so I will have electricity and no longer carry water, chop wood, and put up with my crudities in my manner of living - I am sure it is time to quit - so I will be happy to make the change soon."

One of the last entries of the year was Tuesday December 27, "Flora and I went downtown (to Los Angeles) today and looked at furniture. They are using more handpainted than for several years so I am going to try my skill on some pieces I have. Want to get them ready for the new home."

Flora and her husband did a great deal of traveling and it is probable that they visited the Matterhorn in Switzerland. They may have brought a picture postcard but Mertie made it her own with the addition of redwood trees, stream and cabins. She painted a watercolor of the scene with only one cabin which she evidently made before the quilt.

Only one other quilt, Flora's Quilt, remains in the family. It is both pieced and appliqued. Mertie also painted china and did water colors.

She moved to her new home near Victorville soon after 1955 and there are no more diaries. According to her nephew she became ill and he lost track of her until her attorney notified him of his inheritance. She died October 6, 1966 in San Bernadino, CA.

Her nephew, Melvin Dorsett, wrote to me: "We had been thrilled in her desert home when she pulled back the protective drapes and showed us her textile masterpiece. She did other quilts but this was the only one she created with the hope that 'it would someday be judged worthy of exhibition in a museum' ". Today it is part of the Denver Art Museum quilt collection, a gift of her nephew. He also gave them a copy of her poem:

I quilt with stitches small
And know a century hence
Posterity will gasp and say
How neat.

Jeannette Dean-Throckmorton

Dr. Jeannette Dean-Throckmorton presented five of her quilts to the Art Institute of Chicago for their collection. One of the quilts, the Feathered Star, was lost and there are four in the collection now: Goldfinch and Flowers, dated 1947, Blue Iris, circa 1945, Rosebreasted Grosbeak and State Birds and Flowers.

Jeannette Franc Throckmorton was born at 8 am on Friday January 26, 1883 in Derby, Iowa. She was third in a family of seven children. Her father, Dr. Thomas Throckmorton and her mother, Mary Ann Bentley Throckmorton, were both from large families, so many cousins lived nearby and large family gatherings and much visiting between families occurred. It is probable that much of the social life of that small midwestern community was family oriented. To Jeannette, the family remained an integral part of her life.

Jeannette was a good student and received excellent grades from the public schools in Chariton, Iowa. She performed prodigious feats of memory such as memorizing the Declaration of Independence at the age of twelve and the entire Constitution at the age of fourteen. Her father rewarded her with 25¢ for the first accomplishment and $2.00 for the second. Both events were duly noted in the home town paper and appeared in her genealogy book.

She graduated from Chariton High School and was a speaker at the graduating ceremonies. Her thesis was "The Wisdom of Mother Goose." Unfortunately no copy of that document has survived.

She was most anxious to go to college and was obviously a bright student but she had opposition from her father. Some family members feel that her father only allowed her to go to college after she had promised to go to medical school, enter her father's medical practice, and never marry.

She attended the Simpson College of Liberal Arts and received her Ph.B in June 1904 before attending the Keokuck Medical School where she completed the four year course in three years. She was graduated on May 14, 1907.

When Jeannette took the State Board of Medicine's Examination for a certificate to practice, she received the highest grades of all 140 doctors who were examined by the board. She received a 94% average and 100% in some subjects. These facts were also duly noted in the home town newspaper and clipped for her genealogy book.

1907 was also the year she began quilting.

Dr. Jeannette joined her father's medical practice in 1907 and continued with him until 1919 when her loss of hearing became too much of a problem. She then went into the U.S. Public Health Service and for the next six years she lectured throughout Iowa and nearby states. She lectured on "A Study of the Heredity of Feeblemindness," "Blood Examinations" and "A Preliminary Report on the Health of Women Students in the Colleges of the State."

In 1914 she completed an extensive genealogy about her family, tracing the Throckmorton family back to John Throckmorton who came to this country in 1630. She presented six inch thick books to the members of the six branches of the family. The inscription in each of the books read, "It has been said, the best possessions of a family are its common memories. To honor and preserve the memory of those who have passed to the Great Beyond, to foster a proper family feeling and pride, to keep for the future generations the record of their ancestry, these pages are placed in the hands of the six branches of the family and entrusted to their keeping." Each book was filled with letters, snippets of wedding dresses, photographs, drawings, locks of hair, etc.

In 1916, Dr. Jeannette received a letter from her brother, Dr. Tom Bentley Throckmorton which announced that she had been passed over for office as a member of the State Board of Health. According to "Dr. Tom" the appointment had almost been "air tight" but at the last moment the governor had changed his interpretation of the rules of appointment. Tom wrote, "I almost shed tears today, but I am glad to know I have a sister who at least is known to be better qualified than *any man in the state,* but the failure for Suffrage to carry, and hence your

inability to declare yourself a member of *a* political party, defeated you."
In 1920, Dr. Jeannette was sent to Belgium as a representative of the U.S. Public Health Service and was entertained by the Queen, who herself was an M.D. Later in the same years she was elected Vice President of the Royal Institute of Public Health in England.
On March 1, 1929, (her father deceased) Dr. Jeannette married Dr. Charles N. Dean, a former classmate from Keokuck with whom she had remained friends since graduation. Now aged 46, her photograph in her wedding dress shows the dress to be short and quite elaborate. She wore a head piece and dress length veil which was finished with fringe. Unfortunately the bridegroom became very ill only a few hours after the ceremony and died 10 days later. He was survived by his daughter Jeannette, a child from his first marriage.
On the inside cover of her copy of Marie Webster's book, QUILTS: THEIR STORY AND HOW TO MAKE THEM is the inscription in her handwriting, "Dr. Jeannette Throckmorton-Dean, Sumner, March 11, 1929."
She was extremely proud of her names — both first and last. For sometime after her husband's death she signed her name, "Throckmorton-Dean" but eventually reversed the names and used, "Dean-Throckmorton". She loved to have children named "Jeannette" or "Jean" and was not above applying pressure on family members to do so.
After Dr. Dean's death, Dr. Jeannette took the position of Medical Librarian with the Iowa State Medical Library, and continued to serve in that capacity until her death on July 24, 1963. She enjoyed the position and the young people with whom she associated. She died holding a manuscript of one of the students.
Dr. Jeannette entered her Dogwood quilt in the American Physicians Art Association. They had no "quilt" classification so she entered it in the "tapestry" class. In 1953 there is a letter from the Association congratulating her for the "piece" being voted the most popular by the judges and the finest piece of art work in the whole show. Incidentally she won a cup which had to be shipped to her collect because the treasury of that illustrious group was too low to stand the strain of the freight charges.
She had three books on quilts when she wrote a friend in 1947, but she underlined, annotated, and even drew designs in them all. She wrote names of the recipients of her quilts beside the quilt names and it was not unusual to have four or five names beside a single quilt. Under the picture of the Drunkard's Path in Rose Kretsinger's THE RO-

MANCE OF THE AMERICAN PATCHWORK QUILT she wrote, "I made one for Cousin Merva, Cousin Willa, Clarice Bargor, myself 1950." She wrote "This is a mistake" beside another picture of a Drunkard's Path which showed many slips.

Sometime in the 1950 s, relatives sent her a pamphlet from the Victoria & Albert Museum which showed pictures of quilts donated by an American, Mrs. Foster Stearns. She immediately wrote to the museum asking them if they would be interested in receiving some of her quilts. They replied with a suggestion that she contact the Smithsonian Institution. The Smithsonian policy of not accepting recent works led her to the Chicago Art Institute which was closer to home. Five of her quilts were finally accepted by the museum, two of them in 1959 and three more after Dr. Jeannette's death. In September 1965, a newspaper article shows a picture of one of the five quilts which were on display for the entire month at the museum.

According to her own notes, Dr. Jeannette made many pieced quilts, but she became known for her elaborate applique quilts with stuffed and corded work. Most of them are inscribed with a date and signature and many with the recipient's name. She also used kits, especially for the applique quilts. She didn't use a frame for quilting, but preferred to work on her lap with large sections in a quilt-as-you-go method. In her later years she quilted with her good friend 'Aunt Fanny' Crist. In the summer they quilted at 'Aunt Fanny's' where they could enjoy the garden and birds, but in winter they returned to Dr. Jeannette's where they had electricity and a warmer house.

It isn't known how many quilts she made in her lifetime. Sixteen years before she died, however, she estimated that she had made between 55 and 60. She lost track because she had given so many away.

In a tribute published in Volume 7, Number 2 of NIMBLE NEEDLE TREASURES (1975), Maxine Teele wrote "Long before the phrase had been coined, Dr. Jeannette Franc Dean Throckmorton was a woman's libber in the very best sense. In spite of tragedy and handicaps (deafness plagued her most of her life and her eyesight was greatly impaired in later years) she faced life with zest, optomism, and a complete lack of bitterness. Her accomplishments are remarkable today. When we take into consideration the era in which she was born, they are monumental."

Bertha Stenge

In the 1940's and 1950's Bertha Stenge was a name well known to quilters and quilt lovers. She had won 1st prize at the N.Y. World's Fair, the Grand National Prize at the WOMAN'S DAY National Needlework

Exhibition, had her quilts displayed in one woman shows on both sides of the nation, been interviewed on radio and in newspapers, won scores of blue ribbons in county and state fairs, and her designs and patterns were carried in leading magazines such as WOMAN'S DAY and LADIES' HOME JOURNAL.

Bertha Stenge was born Bertha Sheramsky on February 8, 1891 in Alameda, California, across the bay from San Francisco. Her father later changed the family name to Sheram. She attended Longfellow Grammer School and Alameda High School. It is not clear whether she attended the University of California at Berkeley, but she was a student - possibly a private student - of Eugen Neuhaus, head of the Art Department at U.C.

In 1912 she married Bernard Stenge, an attorney who lived in Chicago. They had three daughters, Frances, Ruth, and Prudence. All three were married, but only Ruth had children. On Mrs. Stenge's death, her quilts were divided between the three daughters. When Ruth died, her share was divided between her three daughters.

Bertha's personal correspondence was carefully filed by the correspondent's city or state. There were many letters from quilters asking for work or replying to Bertha's request for information regarding their fees for quilting and the type of material they would use. Both daughters remember their mother quilting at the frame in the early mornings, so it is likely that she used professional quilters only later in life when she became pressed for time. She hired Mrs. Maud Sielveck of Karnack, Illinois to quilt The Persian Garden, the Victory quilt, and The Quilt Show.

Although Bertha did not begin quiltmaking until her daughters were grown, she won many prizes in state fairs as well as contests. In the 1940 New York World's Fair contest, she entered her Palm Leaf quilt. It won the Grand Prize, and her total earnings for that one show on that one quilt were $725. The quilt was later shown in THE AMERICAN HOME of September 1947 as an advertisement for the pattern.

At the WOMAN'S DAY National Needlework Competition in 1942, Mrs. Stenge won $1,000 - the Grand Award for her Victory quilt - and $125 in additional prizes. The contest was held and then the entries were shown at a large exhibition held at Madison Square Garden with Mary Margaret McBride, a radio celebrity, officiating at the ceremony. It was broadcast over NBC. Mrs. Stenge was invited to the ceremonies as a guest of WOMAN'S DAY. In the March 1943 issue of WOMAN'S DAY, the Victory quilt was pictured in full color. The caption under the picture assured the readers they could reproduce the quilt in cotton materials for about $6.

Thirteen of Bertha Stenge's quilts were hung for a one-woman show at the University of California Art Gallery in 1941. The exhibition was arranged by Mr. Eugen Neuhaus, head of the Art Department, and hung from November ninth to December first. In the summer of 1943, seventeen of her quilts were exhibited at the Art Institute of Chicago. NEWSWEEK of August second carried a review of the show which, according to the correspondence, was a somewhat inaccurate description. Nevertheless, it was a review by a major news publication. It was considered a great success and Mrs. Stenge received a great deal of publicity.

As a result of the publicity she received letters from friends and strangers asking to come to her home to see her quilts. She was extremely generous with them and her personal correspondence is full of letters thanking her for her hospitality and the opportunity to see her wonderful quilts. They frequently mention Bertha's husband and her daughters so it is obvious that "show time" was a family affair.

In November 1953, thirty of her quilts were shown at the Women's International Exposition. Mrs. Stenge was in N.Y. for the week of the show. In 1979, seven of her quilts were exhibited at The Patch in Time Show in San Francisco through the courtesy of her daughters.

In 1971, Mrs. Stenge's daughter Prudence Fuchsman sold some of the quilts, and there was a flurry of articles in the Chicago papers and the quilt publications. Unfortunately, no record was kept of where they went. The Art Institute of Chicago has the quilt Toby Lil in its collections, and the Chicago Historical Society has Chicago Fair. Most of the rest remain in the family.

Bertha Stenge died in Chicago after a brief illness on June 18, 1957. Florence Peto, a personal friend of Bertha's, wrote to her daughter: "The world has lost a magnificent needlewoman; there isn't another with the skill and ingenuity she displayed."

Florence Peto

Florence Peto is the fourth quiltmaker to be discussed. Probably she had the greatest influence on the world of quilting of any of the four women. She was an excellent quiltmaker, wrote extensively, lectured to hundreds of women's groups, influenced museums to buy and exhibit quilts, and she researched the history of some of our best known museum quilts.

She was born Florence Cowdin, one of four children, on November 25, 1881 in New York State. "Florie," as she wanted her children and grandchildren to call her, married Joseph Peto and had two children, John and Marjorie. John and his wife presented her with two grandsons, but Marjorie did not marry, and lived at home with her parents until she died. Marjorie went to Europe during World War II as a lieutenant in the Army Nurse Corps. She later became a captain, and was retired from the Corps as a lieutenant-colonel.

Mrs. Peto was very close to her daughter. When Marjorie died following surgery in 1970, Mrs. Peto took to her bed and never got up again. She died about a year later, aged 88.

Following are excerpts from Florence Peto's letters to Emma Andres between 1939 and 1955. Miss Andres and Mrs. Peto met only once, after many years of corresponding, when Miss Andres was visiting relatives on the East Coast and discovered her "pen pal" actually lived near by.

In the years 1939-43 there were many letters. As the years went by and Mrs. Peto became busier, the letters were less frequent and shorter. But Florence always remember her friend at birthdays, Easter and other holidays. She sent copies of all her writings and many newspaper clippings. Most of the letters are typewritten about every day life but frequently she wrote at length about an antique show or her latest find.

Her first letter to Miss Andres dated April 1, 1939 began, "It was courteous of McCALL'S to send you my address for I enjoyed receiving you letter and am pleased to hear about your hobby. All this began as a hobby with me, too, only I feel now that, after giving thirty-five lectures this winter to Women's Clubs and for the Board of Education to their textile arts groups — well, it has outgrown the hobby stage.

My photographs of American-made quilts, spreads and woven coverlets number over three hundred - all have authentic histories verified by family records and papers... what I desire to do in gathering this material (is to) preserve the memory and identity of the quiltmaker as well as her needlework."

On May 24, 1940 Mrs. Peto wrote "Well I lived through another broadcast experience... the subject was 'Friendship and Album quilts'. An announcer asked all the questions and I had all the answers! The Index of American Design for whom I gave the broadcast have given me a lot of photographs of quilts, some of them most unusual. Now I have a lot of research to do for there were no histories for them."

On August 13, a letter stated, "...Am to repeat my lecture at the World's Fair; the Index of American Design considered it so successful they want to throw another 'Quilting Bee'. '

March 21, 1941: "You are right; they keep me talking and talking. It is wonder someone hasn't popped me into the U.S. Senate — the only place where there is more talking than I do! Next week, I give two more lectures and again one on the 26th. So when you do not hear from me, picture me with my mouth open."

June 3, 1941: "For two days before Memorial Day, I gave out and lay flat on my back in bed; suppose I was overdoing it with all that work in such awful hot weather... Was enough better yesterday to hobble over to town and get my hair done — because I had decided that even if I was going to die I could not die with hair in such a mess as mine was! I felt very sorry for myself. Got a new permanent - a short hair cut and now have curls all over my pate and look as nearly like Shirley Temple as I ever will!"

June 6th, 1941, "Maybe it was to pay me back for the Shirley Temple hair-do that I have been ill in bed most of the time since."

June 13, 1941, "My husband is funny: he can cook fairly well and clean up pretty well but there won't be a dish left if I don't get around soon! He comes upstairs like a small boy after I've heard a crash and tries to say that he didn't do it — it slips from some place or bounces without anyone being near it — so help him."

December 8, 1942, "The fun of Christmas is halted with the awful news over the radio last night; we were visiting friends in Brooklyn and we all sat as if stunned when we heard the news and realized the perfidy of Japan. Who knows what may be ahead.

Must go and make a pudding now — we have to eat no matter how sad and worried. Maybe I'll get out my nine-patch quilt and try to finish it — practise what I preach. Good to keep busy when you are in trouble or worried."

February 26, 1942, "After I put my aunt on her train yesterday in N.Y. I wandered into the stores; it was fatal for I bought two new dresses and a red, red hat! I was feeling rather 'down' and thought it might cheer me up to have some new clothes. I'm usually very conservative about what I wear on the platform but the next group listening to me is going to have to look at a red bonnet! I hope there will be no bulls among them."

February 6, 1942, "Well the lightning has struck; daughter Marjorie goes away next Tuesday. I cannot imagine my life without her gay and loving personality about. She has been such a good child; how I hope she can be of service to her country and yet not have to undergo too many cruel hardships herself."

February 15, 1942, "More dead than alive after a week of the most emotional upset; my daughter finally got away this morning. I did not go over to N.Y. to say 'Goodby' for I felt one more Goodby would finish me. Well, that's that; I simply cannot cry anymore. My heart is so leaden you could make bullets out of it. We didn't cry when we parted her though- we laughed - she is the grandest girl to have laughs with!

January 18, 1944, "News: I finished my Nine-Patch quilt-top yesterday; now, the border and then I shall send it away to be quilted. It is so pretty."

February 13, 1945, "My friend in Ohio, who gave my nine-patch out to be quilted, wrote that it is all done but the binding."

September 11, 1945, "We have had such thrilling news: Marjorie is on her way home! She is to sail from Marseilles on September 15. The house is being scrubbed until the paint comes off!"

December 2, 1945, "Since Marjorie came home this house has been in such a whirl I've had no time for my own affairs and, indeed, owe everyone I know a letter."

January 4, 1955, "Guess what Marjorie gave me? Sure, a quilt! A beautiful 'Cockscomb & Currants,' exquisitely quilted! It was fun to see the children of the family on Christmas afternoon when we rode over to my son's."

Mrs. Peto liked to enter her quilts in contests and state fairs. Evidently she sometimes entered the same contests as Bertha Stenge though in different classifications. She sent a quilt to the contest at the Eastern States Exposition as late as 1967, three years before her death. She wrote a friend on November 28, 1967, "The work on some of the antique pieces will never be duplicated but it is far from a 'lost art'. 'Lost art of quilting' — indeed — there is excellent work being done commercially and privately even by myself and I've a bureau drawer full of ribbons to prove it."

Quilts from her antique collection were frequently on display. In 1948, the N.Y. Historical Society had an exhibition of quilts. A newspaper article states that it included Mrs. Peto's "entire collection of 50 quilts". In 1955 the Henry Ford Museum had an exhibit of her quilts. On December 12, 1967, she wrote to a friend, "Now I am getting ready for the big Exhibition of my whole quilt collection in the Suffolk County Museum in Stony Brook, L.I. It will go from Jan. 23 to April 23. This will be the last time I will show quilts as a collection for, after the show, I mean to offer many of them for sale. I have already sold some. I need the storage space."

On February 17, 1968 she wrote the same friend, "I... have taken apart my lecture chart which I used to illustrate my Quilt Talk. There were 45 quilt blocks - hand made by me of course and in colors that would project from the platform. Now I am having pillows made of several and our local Woman's Exchange sells them as fast as I get them made. They are attractive and different. But I feel as if I were betraying old friends."

In the '60's Florence Peto launched another career. She began giving classes, writing articles, and designing kits for crewel embroidery. She didn't forsake her interst in quilts and historical textiles, she just added another full time interest. She frequently complained about being tired, but she loved the activity and complained just as bitterly if she had to give up something because of ill health.

Florence Peto died August 29, 1970. What a full life she led and what a wonderful heritage she left us! There are many quilts in museums because of her interst. Four of the most famous are the Emeline Dean quilt and the Demarest Medley in the Newark Museum, Mary Totten's Rising Sun in the Smithsonian Institution, and Sophonisba Peale's Star Medallion in the Philadelphia Museum of Art.

These are but four of the large number of "fine" quiltmakers of the 1940's and 50's. Their names are well known to most of us, not necessarily because they are the best but because they have quilts in museum collections. There are many more who deserve the same honor.

Quilts in Pomo Culture*

Sandra J. Metzler-Smith

California is noted for the exceptional basketry traditions of its Native American peoples. Among these, the baskets of the Pomo have the name of being the finest made in California, if not the world.[1] Pomo basketry is an art form in which color of materials, shape, design, texture and fineness of weave are manipulated for ends that are purely aesthetic as well as practical. Adept with their hands, Pomo women basketweavers admired and quickly duplicated the colorful patchwork quilts of the early white settlers in Mendocino County. What is the nature of these quilts and the Hopland Friendship Quilt of 1928 in particular?

Pomo baskets are not made by a single tribe of Native Americans but rather by members of some seventy-two autonomous groups living in the North Coast Range of California. Seven distinct but related languages were spoken, six of which had a number of dialects. Anthropologists have assigned names to these linguistic groups according to their relative geographical location: Northern Pomo, Central Pomo, Southern Pomo, Southwestern Pomo, Northwestern Pomo, Eastern Pomo, and Southeastern Pomo.[2]

Although the linguistic groups did not perceive of themselves as a homogeneous group, they did have a number of features in common. All lived in large, permanent villages that were mutually linked by marriage, trade and ceremonies. All drew their subsistence from fishing, gathering and hunting. In addition, all shared a common expertise and similar technology for the making of various types of basketry.[3]

Because of their rich environment which gave them bountiful

Sandra J. Metzler-Smith, BA, University of California, is Curator of the Mendocino County Museum. Her post-graduate studies in textiles have included documentation, preservation social significance, and research in wool. She has curated nine quilt exhibitions and raises Black Romney sheep for handspinning fleeces. Address: Mendocino County Museum, 400 E. Commercial St., Willits, CA 95490.

*Copyright 1980 Mendocino County Museum.

harvests of fish and acorns, the Pomo led a more sedentary life than other nonagriculturalists, presumably freeing their time for expanding the aesthetic dimension of basket production. The men generally performed the coarser labor of openwork twining such as traps and cradles which, as A.L. Kroeber states, relieved the women of "this dull and heavy practical industry" to stimulate them "to attempt the achievement of a true art."[4]

During the nineteenth century, the various Pomo groups came into permanent contact with members of European society. The Russians, Spanish and Mexicans all had their impact early but it was not until the 1850s when California had become a state that the Pomo were pushed from their lands. Two reservations were formed in Mendocino County to centralize the Indians, one of which, Round Valley, still exists today. Thus acculturation began with the attempts of the Pomo people to survive in a new world.

One significant impact on the traditional Pomo culture was the realization by the women that their crafts had a cash value and they began to manufacture baskets specifically for sale. By the 1890s, there was a brisk business conducted by professional basket buyers who made semiannual trips into Northern California to purchase baskets.[5]

A second means of adapting to the new culture was as agricultural labor which provided cash for the new commodities available in the white towns. Harvesting crops, such as hops, became the sole livelihood for many Pomo between 1880 and 1940.[6]

Besides hop-picking, the Pomo women had an alternative source for employment. Some of them worked for the white townspeople where they would "do a days worth of laundry for twenty-five cents."[7] Ellen Wood, a Pomo woman, recalled in 1940: "My aunt . . . makes beads and makes baskets, and she do all the things . . . And she go around among white people to wash. And that's how I learn to wash."[8]

The town of Hopland was named in the days when the hop, the ingredient giving beer its bitter flavor, was Mendocino County's leading crop. Once, hops could be seen greening fields all over the county. Now they can only occasionally be viewed growing wild along the fences bordering fields where they have been replaced by grapes and pears.[9]

Hopland was also the site of an Indian "rancheria," isolated small acreages held in protective trust by the United States since the turn of the century.[10] The Hopland Rancheria consisted originally of some 2,070 acres and had a school for the Indian children. It is here that the "Hopland Friendship Quilt" was made in 1928.

In a letter from the donor of the quilt to the Mendocino County

Museum when it was added to the permanent collection in 1974, Geraldine Youd stated:

> Around fifty years ago I commenced teaching in the Hopland Elementary School. The first five years of the seventeen years I was there, I lived on the rancheria with the various teachers and drove back and forth to the little town of Hopland. The Indians seemed to hold us at arm's length. To gain their confidence, one of the teachers (Eunice Davies) and I decided to have them help us make the quilt that I am mailing you. I bought the materials and placed the designs on the squares of chambray, and invited both the women and men to come to the teacherage where we lived in the evenings. They were quite responsive and were soon handling an embroidery needle as if they had always used one. You will notice the signatures on the block each made, is authentic, and makes the quilt more valuable. My signature is on the last block. We found them to be very fine people, and we became real good friends.[11]

Who were the Indians that participated in the Friendship Quilt? Some were children like Ignatius Billy who later graduated from the University of California and worked for the BIA in Washington, D.C., or Blanch Knight who now lives in Cloverdale. Some were men, such as J.A. Knight, the brother of Blanch, who served in World War I. With "Jensie" Knight's embroidered quilt block, the entire Knight family is represented. Still other contributors were adults at the time who particpated with their children, like Evelyn Joaquin. Three of the women, S. Bartlett (or Salome Bartlett Alcantro), Alice Elliott and Elsie Allen are today accomplished basketweavers.

As Elsie Allen recalls, each person who knew the teacher, Mrs. Mudd, received a block to take home and embroider. The blocks were already stenciled and the individuals were told "just sew." Mrs. Allen remembers that the project "sounded interesting so everybody did it."[12] There were no friendship quilts before so the idea was innovative and inviting to the participants.

The stencils, depicting colonial themes and Eastern Plains Indians scenes, had no meaning to the Pomo and still have none. "Indian Home Life," "Indian," "King Phillip," "Pocahontas-Smith" and "Standish Answers Indians" are all images that are as foreign to the California Indians as scenes of China or Alaska.

Coiling a basket is not unlike sewing a quilt: it is a time-consuming process which begins with the collection of the appropriate materials and is constructed with advance knowledge of its intended function, shape and design. The Pomo employ two coiling techniques: one-rod or stick and three-rod or stick. The main difference between the finished products of these two methods is that in one-rod coiling the vessel walls are smoother. Three-rod coiling, on the other hand, has the advantage in that it lends itself to the addition of feathers as decorative elements.

The tool kit of a Pomo basketweaver of about 150 years ago would have included a basket in which to soak the materials, an obsidian knife with which to shape the fibers and a bone awl made from a deer fibula.[13] By the 1870s, the tool kit had become what it is today: a pan of water, a piece of broken glass or a bit of broken knife, a sharp pair of scissors or a single-edge razor blade and a steel awl set in a wooden handle. A No. 18 yarn darning needle or a No. 13 tapestry needle is also recommended.[14] These are used to separate the spaces between each coiled root of sedge and willow to make it easier to stitch the thread-like root. Like quilts, Pomo baskets are judged by the evenness and number of stitches per inch, the finest being about 65-120 stitches per inch. Through time, the baskets by one weaver can be seen decreasing in size while increasing in fineness of stitch.

Designs in black bulrush root or dark brown redbud bark are repetitive geometric motifs. Coiled baskets, because they are circular in construction, have horizontal, diagonal, crossing, radiating or isolated arrangements. The effect is often one of movement and flight.

In the AUTOBIOGRAPHIES OF THREE POMO WOMEN by Elizabeth Colson consisting of information gathered as "life histories" in 1939, 1940, and 1941 from women in their late sixties, "Jane Adams" states:

> My mother good hand at baskets. She teach me how to fix the basket roots, and how to work on it. Just the way you going to do, make it like this, she tell me. (Did you learn to make anything else?) Well, they got nothing to make. They got nothing to teach. That's all the work they had, the baskets. But nowadays they crochet, like that. Everything they learn in school. Patchwork quilt. That why they don't want to work on basket. Easier to crochet. They can buy the thread. Basket roots they have to get out and take. That's hard work, not very easy. And gathering willow — that's kind of hard for young girls now. They dressed up, and basket root digging is awful dirty job.[15]

Two Pomo women born near the turn of the century were recently interviewed. Although their information varied slightly in fine detail, they both provide insights into the Pomo artisan — basketmaker/

quiltmaker. How was quiltmaking introduced into Pomo culture? Both women believe their people were good at copying what they saw. Because a Pomo woman was often employed by a white family to wash clothes, she handled and studied the construction of a quilt. "Good with their hands" from weaving baskets, the women found little difficulty in handsewing. Furthermore, it simply "did not take long to learn to grasp the white culture."[16]

It was explained that some wealthy white families would "adopt" certain Pomo families as friends. Often they would bring food and used clothing to the rancherias. The Pomo, in turn reciprocated with gifts, usually baskets. Men's old woolen suits or out-dated ladies' dresses "were not their style" so "they would tear them up to make into quilts."[17]

Practicality and beauty were both important. Overalls that had torn were sewn into utility quilts or ground blankets and taken to the hopfields. Hop-pickers and their families slept on a pile of straw with a layer of cotton blankets and quilts.[18]

Satins and silks, on the other hand, were also treasured. In Potter Valley, for example, the Pomo quiltmakers "competed with one another" for who had the lovelier quilt.[19] This prestige and pride is traditionally found with competing basketmakers as well.

Designs for quilts were geometric, most commonly squares. No applique quilts are known to have been made by the Pomo. Patterns were never from books. One quiltmaker believed that "you lose pattern in mind if use book" so both basket and quilt designs were imbedded in the creative mind of the maker.[20] Sharing of the patterns among the Pomo was common. Because basketmakers and quiltmakers always worked alone traditionally sitting on the floor to weave or sew, they were private with their work. But after hop-picking time, the quilts would be washed and hung on the clothesline to dry where all the women would see and admire the show. One woman remembers how they would "ooh and aah" over the colorful exhibition.[21] If there was a pattern that a quiltmaker particularly liked, she would study it at a distance and then go home to duplicate it. "Eyes were so sharp, memories so good, they just remembered."[22]

By the 1870s, patchwork quilts were commonly made by the Pomo Indians of Mendocino County. It was also established by this time that a good basketweaver made a good quiltmaker. In fact, in Pomo language, the terms are synonymous: a woman is described as "ta na sha" or "the hands know, knowing hands."[23]

The quilt itself has a Pomo name, "sha tzun," meaning "heavier and thicker" than blanket or "bah tah." These words are most likely from the earlier terms for animal pelt blankets, the thick and heavy animal hide like bear and a thinner blanket like a deer pelt.

Pomo women found the making of quilts an appealing part of white culture. Whether it was for practical use in the hopfields or for prestige in competing with a neighbor, the finest quilts were made by the deft fingers of the Pomo basketweaver. Although the Hopland Friendship Quilt may be an exception, it is an important historic document for Mendocino County. As one Pomo woman expressed: "So much basket. Sew and quilt, then go back to baskets... weaving is tedious, quilting relaxes."[25]

Notes:

1. Alfred Louis Kroeber, HANDBOOK OF THE INDIANS OF CALIFORNIA, San Francisco: California Book Company, 1925, p. 244.
2. S.A. Barrett, POMO INDIAN BASKETRY, University of California Publications in American Archaeology and Ethnology, Vol. 7, No. 3, Berkeley: University of California Press, 1908 pp. 134-308.
3. Anna Curtenius Roosevelt and James G.E. Smith, THE ANCESTORS, New York: The Museum of the American Indian, 1979, p. 107.
4. Kroeber, HANDBOOK, p. 246.
5. Roosevelt and Smith, ANCESTORS, p. 110.
6. Thomas C. Owens, THE YOKAIA, Ukiah: Mendocino Historical Society, 1980, p. 20.
7. Ethel Docker, THE GOOD OLD DAYS, San Francisco: Panpipes Publications, 1968, p. 14.
8. Elizabeth Colson, AUTOBIOGRAPHIES OF THREE POMO WOMEN, Berkeley: Archaeological Research Facility, Department of Anthropology, 1974, p. 136.
9. Ted Erickson Jr., "County's Hops: Once King, now a Pauper Weed," Ukiah, The Ukiah Daily Journal, October 5, 1980, p. 11.

10. Final Report of State Advisory Commission of Indian Affairs, 1969, p. 9.
11. Accession Records (74-13-1), Willits Mendocino County Museum.
12. Interview with Elsie Allen, 4/15/80, Willits, Mendocino County Museum.
13. Roosevelt & Smith, ANCESTORS, p. 121.
14. Sandra Conie Newman, INDIAN BASKET WEAVING, Flagstaff: Northland Press 1974, p. 11.
15. Elizabeth Colson, AUTOBIOGRAPHIES OF THREE POMO WOMEN, pp. 201-202.
16. Interview - Elsie Allen, 4/15/80 Mendocino County Museum.
17. Personal interview, 10/24/80, between author and Pomo informant, Willits, Mendocino County Museum.
18. Person l interview, 5/12/80, between author and Pomo informant, Willits, Mendocino County Museum.
19. Ibid.
20. Personal interview, 4/15/80 between Pomo informant and author, Willits, Mendocino County Museum.
21. Ibid.
22. Personal interview, 5/12/80, Willits, Mendocino County Museum.
23. Personal interview, 9/11/80, word from one Northern Pomo dialect
24. Personal interview, 10/24/80, words are from one Northern Pomo dialect.
25. Personal interview, 4/15/80, between author and Pomo informant, Willits, Mendocino County Museum.

Design Invention in Country Quilts of Tennessee and Georgia

Bets Ramsey

My involvement with quilts began in 1971 when I did a graduate research paper on American quilts. The topic was selected from a list of suitable subjects because it was the closest to my own area of work —stitchery and fabric collage. I tried to read every book available in Tennessee and in the Library of Congress on the subject of quilts. Incidentally, at the LC I was excited to find a vast number of catalog cards headed "patchwork" which disappointingly turned out to be collections of Victorian verse and short prose.

My project was further implemented by interviews with elderly relatives and persons who were well acquainted with quiltmaking and collecting. Because I grew up in another part of the country I was unaware of my Georgia family heritage of splendid needlework. I took great pleasure in discovering my unknown ancestors through my quilt study. I gathered up family quilts and continued to collect stories and slides while my own efforts at quiltmaking slowly progressed.

From the first, my interest centered on the simple country quilts which possessed some unexpected turn or use of fabric. I was finding the same elements of design, the same sparks of invention in Appalachian quilts that Jonathan Holstein and Gail van der Hoof were discovering in quilts of the Northeast. The honest beauty and directness pleased me. I felt obligated to save these everyday quilts from relegation to moving pads and stadium blankets. I felt a duty to future historians. Then, too, my budget could afford the quilts that no one else prized.

> Bets Ramsey, MS, University of Tennessee, is Visual Arts Director of the Neighbors of Chattanooga, Instructor at Arrowmont, and Director of the Southern Quilt Symposium affiliated with the Hunter Museum of Art. She has exhibited her textile art widely, and written about quilts for CRAFT HORIZONS and YANKEE MAGAZINE. Address: Box 4146, Chattanooga, TN 37405.

DESIGN INVENTION IN COUNTRY QUILTS

What most exemplifies the southern country quilt? I propose that a limitation of material has direct bearing on the total design of the quilt. Because of restriction more improvisation takes place. The easy out is not available. Substitution must be made. Compromise and adaptations are worked out. An artist sets a problem and, working within certain boundaries, goes about solving it to the best of his or her ability. To my way of thinking, the quiltmaker with a narrow limitation of material is operating within a similar framework.

One of my earliest interviews was with Susie Atkins, a neighbor of Charles Counts, the potter and quiltmaker. She was reputed to have the most beautiful quilt on the back of Lookout Mountain (Georgia) and the reputation was well deserved. Mrs. Atkins showed me a magnificent quilt, with elaborate stitching and stuffing, made by her great-grandmother about 1800. It was of dark blue dotted calico and white in a pattern she called True Lover's Knot, also known as Whig's Defeat. It is an elegant quilt with grace and beauty and superb workmanship.

"I've been offered $500 for this quilt," Mrs. Atkins said (before inflation), "but I wouldn't take anything for it. It's been in our family too long. We don't quilt like that any more!"

Then she showed me the quilt she was completing for her granddaughter's wedding, one called Blue Change. The stitches were even and smooth, but not the equal of her great-grandma's, and the choice of fabric was tasteless.

I asked Charles why, when she had so much appreciation for her family treasure, she turned out one of such mundane quality.

"It is a matter of choice," Charles said. "In the old days you bought a little cloth from the peddlar wagon or the general store and made do with what you had. Now the ladies go into the yard-goods supermarkets and lose their heads with the unlimited choices. Some of the sensitivity has been lost. The products aren't as good any more."

The matter of choice is at the center of my study of the country quilt. Choice may be governed by restriction and limitation.

The eager new quilter is in the dilemma of choice as she selects expensive reproduction calico to color-coordinate in her suburban home. The nice material is cut into little pieces and sewn back together again as directed in the magazine. We can expect to find few surprises in the finished product. Compromise is virtually unknown.

There was devastation in the South after The (Civil) War. There was poverty and a need for frugal living. Fortunately the near self-sufficiency of the southern rural population provided a healing atmosphere for recovery. The quiltmakers, as required, used the resources at hand. Everyday tops were pieced of dress scraps, printed

T. Fred Miller

Susie Atkins shows author her prized quilt. Lookout Mountain, Georgia, 1973

DESIGN INVENTION IN COUNTRY QUILTS

flour sacks, unworn parts of garments, home-dyed domestic, and a minimum of new fabric. Backing material was equally varied. If the cost of cotton-checks or domestic was prohibitive, the quilter improvised with feed sacks, homespun, patchwork of used garments, or even nickel-bag tobacco sacks pieced together. In most instances cotton for filler was readily available, — simply plant it, grow it, pick it, take it to gin, and card it into batts.

Do not imagine that all southern families were poor dirt farmers. By today's standards their cash incomes seem pitifully small, but most rural families had comfortable farms, large families, and plenty to eat. They knew how to make the most of what they had. They were not inhibited by fashion. Their attributes of spirit and adventure are reflected in their quilts.

The following limitations, variations, and inventions have been observed in my study of country quilts of Tennessee and Georgia.

The Sally Hobbs Quilt, made in Brunswick County, Virginia in 1790 and eventually brought to Tennessee, uses cut-outs of rare imported fabrics applied to a background of less costly yardage. By combining

T. Fred Miller

The joy of the misplaced pieces. Ocean Waves quilt top, circa 1900. Chattanooga, TN.

the scarce with the available cloth the maker handled her materials wisely and well. Similar examples from the period are to be found in museums and historic houses.[1]

Settlers who moved into the southern highlands of the Carolinas and Tennessee in the early 1800's replaced the imported calicos in their quilts with floral cut-outs made from home-dyed fabric. The motifs are bolder, more stylized than those from the lowlands, as seen in several examples in the Z.C. and Sara Key Patten Collection.[2]

A few choice pieces of roller-print are combined with common material in a splendidly simple basket of Carolina lilies. The smallest fragments and scraps of rich material are thus used to great advantage.[3]

In the deep south, near Athens, Georgia for example, a regional style developed which is characterized by extensive use of white heightened with lesser amounts of color and print. Formal elegance is noted in these quilts which appear cool rather than warm and comforting.[4]

A certain richness such as one finds in an Oriental rug is achieved in the use of unmatched colors and textures. The Log Cabin pattern made of numerous scraps has a syncopated, unexpected rhythm caused by the shifting of color and intensity. It is a sensation which cannot be accomplished in a carefully planned quilt.[5]

Small quilt-tops or fragments extended with borders acquire a totally different setting from the top that has little or no border. The sensitive quiltmaker finishes her quilt with a frame, a proper border. The lack of such treatment can be disturbing.[6]

Natural dyeing was a practical as well as an esthetic consideration. In addition to the turkey red and copperas dyeing for brilliant color, there was natural dyeing with walnut, maple, oak, sumac, broomsedge, dock, scotchbroom, bloodroot, ladies' bedstraw, and, of course, indigo. Domestic (unbleached muslin) for background and lining when boiled with red clay dirt and water took on a rosy glow which did not show the soil (no pun intended) as soon as a light quilt. Walnut hulls were used to color a white quilt-back that would otherwise have appeared dingy in limestone-water washings.[7]

The country quilt ladies who made quilts from their scrap bags frequently joined one piece to another without consideration for organization. It is in this unexpected juxtaposition of colors and values that one finds entertainment for the eye. The movement jumps from one dominant spot to another and back and around, then rests for a moment in a quiet area before finding new paths to follow. The unplanned course is fresh and appealing.[8]

The same sort of eye movement occurs in looking at quilts of regular, symmetrical pattern when there is a change of intensity and hue. The flatness and dull repetition are enlivened when the fabrics mix and flow in pleasing variation.[9]

Perhaps the string quilt is the epitome of quiltmaking economy when the ragtag ends and bits of material are used to make units for a block. The process involves a great deal of time, no economy there, and without careful planning the overall design may fall far short of success. Those country quilters with a sense of design have made some noteworthy quilts in string quilt technique.[10]

A certain surprise element is present in a misplaced piece, whether deliberate or accidental. A small allover pattern such as Ocean Waves arrests attention when occasional triangles are upside down or sideways. We may take the quilter to task for failing to correct her mistakes but, for me, I find joy and relief in the misplaced piece.[11]

T. Fred Miller

Lola Fitzgerald and Freddie Mae Woods prepare to air their scrap-bag quilts. Hixson, TN. 1975

If the same care is given to designing borders and joinings that is given to making blocks, the products of quiltmaking would be tremendously improved. As it is, most quilts have been put together with dull strips and little or no border. When an interesting setting is discovered, it is time to sit up and take notice. An original treatment at the intersection of stripping adds spice to the block. Sometimes two colors have been joined in bands for stripping. Invention is welcome in borders, sashing, and joining units to enhance the design and alleviate boredom.[12]

There may be accidental beauty in unmatched backgrounds and mismatched pieces, as in the quilts of Lillian Beattie who sometimes runs out of background fabric for her appliqued figures. She uses the nearest match which may be a few shades off, but adds rather than detracts from the composition.[13]

Perhaps the average eye has rejected the plain, country quilt because of a lack of understanding of its purpose and making. The personal statement is there, if one looks for it and does not feel compelled to make comparisons with grander works. With study and comprehension come empathy.

We weep at the humblest quilts made from bits and scraps, bottoms of men's pants legs, nickel-bag tobacco sacks, sock tops.

We cherish the feel of the handspun, handwoven quilt-back.

We admire the patience of the quilt stuffer.

We smile at the invention in filling a large space.

We acknowledge the finality made at the corner of a quilt.

These southern quiltmakers had originality, persistence, skill, pride, the desire for something beautiful. They possessed the willingness to make quilts for necessity. They made quilts for pleasure and for love.

DESIGN INVENTION IN COUNTRY QUILTS 55

Notes

1. Mrs. W.J. Hagan, Jr. of Lookout Mt., TN recently donated this quilt to the Birmingham (Alabama) Museum.
2. Z. C. and Sarah Key Patten Collection, Ashland Farm near Chattanooga, TN.
3. Ibid. Thought to have been made near Lenoir City, TN c. 1850.
4. Various quilts shown in the collection and gatherings of Dr. Roy Ward, Watkinsville, GA.
5. Examples are numerous and include those from the author's collection; the exhibition Log Cabin and String Quilts, the Hunter Museum, Chattanooga, TN, 1979; and quilts by members of Senior Neighbors of Chattanooga, Inc.
6. Melissa Thompson, Nolensville, TN, extended a small Log Cabin quilt with a series of three borders for a "short cut to the Log Cabin." An excellent treatise on borders is found in Dr. William R. Dunton's book, OLD QUILTS.
7. Dot Davis, Hixson, TN, showed a string quilt dyed with red clay. According to Lola Fitzgerald, also of Hixson, her mother colored her quilt-backs with walnut dye because of the heavy limestone content of the water supply at Cloud Spring, GA, which precluded a "white" wash.
8. A nine patch quilt made by the artist Alma Lesch at the age of five has unexpected relationships and the same whimsy as in her later works. The author has a number of scrap quilts in her collection.
9. Dutch Rose quilt by Hattie Bryant, Chattanooga, is an excellent example, made c. 1955.
10. Lillie Johnson of Chattanooga owns a Bay Leaf quilt made by her grandmother c. 1890. The leaves made in string-strips are so regular they appear to be made of striped material.
11. Ocean Waves quilt c. 1900 belonging to author.
12. In particular, Dutch Flower Pot quilt, Dr. Roy Ward.
13. Lillian Beattie, a 100 year-old lady who appliques lively cloth figures derived from magazine and newspaper illustrations.

Pieced Lettering on Seven Quilts Dating From 1833 to 1891

Winifred Reddall

Very few quilts with pieced lettering have come to light, up to the present time. A prodigious example was discovered in 1979 and exhibited at "Patch in Time #4" in San Francisco. It was number 38 in the catalogue of that show, under the title "Quotation Quilt". Its design is entirely a lettered message pieced of red calico and natural muslin rectangles. The central message reads: "& FROM EVERY QUARTER FLOWING JOYFUL CROWDS ASSEMBLE ROUND AND SPAKE WITH EXALTED ZEAL". The border contains a benediction: "May the blessing of God await thee," with the name of the maker: "Cornelia Catherine Vosburgh" and the date and location: "Red Hook Dec, 25 1874." (Red Hook is in the state of New York.) This quilt is now the cherished possession of a great-grandson of the maker, living in northern California.

The Vosburgh quilt is a masterpiece of its kind; it warrants a study of its lettering style, and an effort to trace the source of its message. It provokes a number of questions: What prompted Cornelia to make a lettered quilt? Was she inspired by other lettered quilts? Did she use a pattern for the letters or design them herself?

A search of the literature turned up six other 19th century quilts whose monograms or messages display the same general style of lettering. Simply listing the origins of these quilts revealed a regional identity for the group. Documentation indicates that four of the seven quilts were made in upstate New York: the Vosburgh quilt from Red Hook[1], the Wildman and Waldron quilts from Castile[2,3], and the Covel quilt from Canandaigua[5]. One of the seven — the Woodhouse quilt — is from Newark, New Jersey[7], another, initialed "J.S.", is from Con-

---

Winifred Reddall, BA, University of California, is a research assistant for QUILTERS' JOURNAL, and a charter member of the Santa Rosa Quilt Guild. She has been an active genealogist for many years and was editor of a genealogical magazine. Address: 1631 Tahoe Dr., Santa Rosa, CA 95405.

VOSBURGH QUILT

photo — Kokomo Print Works

necticut[6]. The seventh, made by Maria Cadman Hubbard, is described as of "probable" New England origin[4]. This clustering in the northeastern section of the country has no ready explanation.

Five of these quilts pre-date the Vosburgh quilt, so a possibility exists that Cornelia had viewed one or more of these lettered quilts — perhaps at a County Fair or an Agricultural show. These occasions afforded exhibitions of women's handiwork, although the meager newspaper reports do not make it clear whether quilts were part of the show. It is logical to assume that 100 years ago more lettered quilts existed than do now survive, which increases the possibility the Cornelia could have seen an example, not necessarily one of those now under consideration —perhaps one pieced by a relative or friend.

How closely Cornelia's lettering resembles these others can best be seen by comparing the variations on each letter of the alphabet in turn, as exhibited on all 7 quilts. Only the "upper case" or "capital" letters were used on 5 of the quilts, so the comparison is confined to these (See Appendix). It should be noted that all the letters are 7 units, or 7 "blocks" in height. Their widths vary from 3 units, (letter "I") to 15 units (for an oversized letter "W" on the Waldron Quilt, which may be a mistake in piecing — deliberate or otherwise — so awkwardly is it fashioned.) The descendants of Cornelia Vosburgh believed her message was a Bible quotation, but a careful search of Concordances by several Bible scholars has failed to find a trace of such a quotation, although its Christian emphasis is not in dispute. It has also been likened to the style of PILGRIM'S PROGRESS and to the style of many fervent hymns, but these possibilites cannot be easily traced, lacking the indexing of Bible passages.

The comparison of letters A to Z on all these quilts revealed the wholly unexpected fact that *every* letter of the alphabet occurs in the 14-word central message of the Vosburgh quilt. This seemed very unusual, so, as a comparison, the content of the Hubbard quilt was examined. Its many short, pious messages contained an even 100 words in all, yet these many words still did not include the entire alphabet. The letters J, Q, X, and Z were missing.

So the question arose: How unusual is it for a 14-word phrase or sentence to contain every letter of the alphabet? This led to more extensive comparisons, the analysis of an additional 20 phrases, all 14 words long, chosen for their religious or philosophical slant, using longer words than the Hubbard quilt — indeed, as nearly as possible of similar context to the Vosburgh message. Five of the phrases were from the Bible, five from the Book of Common Prayer, two from the Koran, three from Pilgrim's Progress, and one each from Shakespeare, Dryden, Defoe, Congreve and Johnson. None of these 14-word phrases contained every letter of the alphabet. Every phrase lacked from 5 to 10 letters. Considering the entire group of phrases, 280 words in all (20 x 14), two letters of the alphabet (x and z) did not appear in any of them. Yet both of these rare letters appeared in Cornelia's 14 words.

Based on the foregoing, it appears probable that Cornelia Catharine Vosburgh had several motives for making this quilt: It is an obvious expression of her Christian faith, proclaimed in a lasting form. And now it seems likely that she also wanted to execute and preserve an entire pieced alphabet from A to Z. The fact that her message includes all 26 letters of the alphabet in a mere 14 words can hardly be considered coincidence. One can only conclude that it was carefully planned within her remarkable paraphrasing of the Coming of Christ.

If the style of the pieced letters seems familiar one need look no further than the samplers dating around 1800, to find the same lettering formations.[8, 9] These sampler alphabets, with their letters formed of cross-stitched or satin-stitched "squares", were intended to be used as patterns for future projects. Cornelia Vosburgh's letters so closely follow the "classic" sampler alphabet that she almost certainly used such a guide or pattern. It may well be that her sampler was old and disintegrating, needing to be replaced by the giant sampler that her quilt became, preserving the letters for another century or two.

Appendix:

PIECED LETTER VARIATIONS IN SEVEN QUILTS
FROM 1833 - 1891

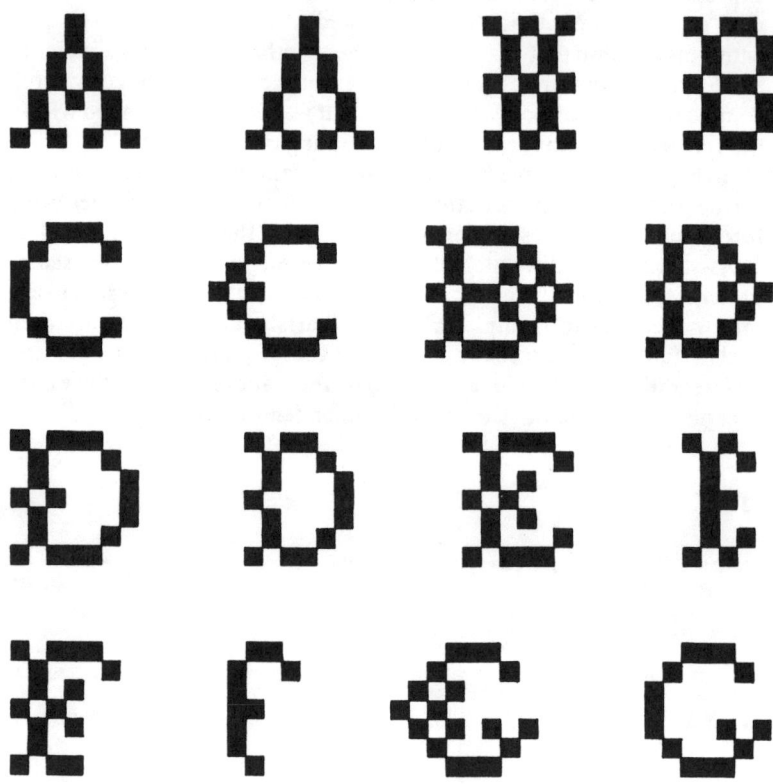

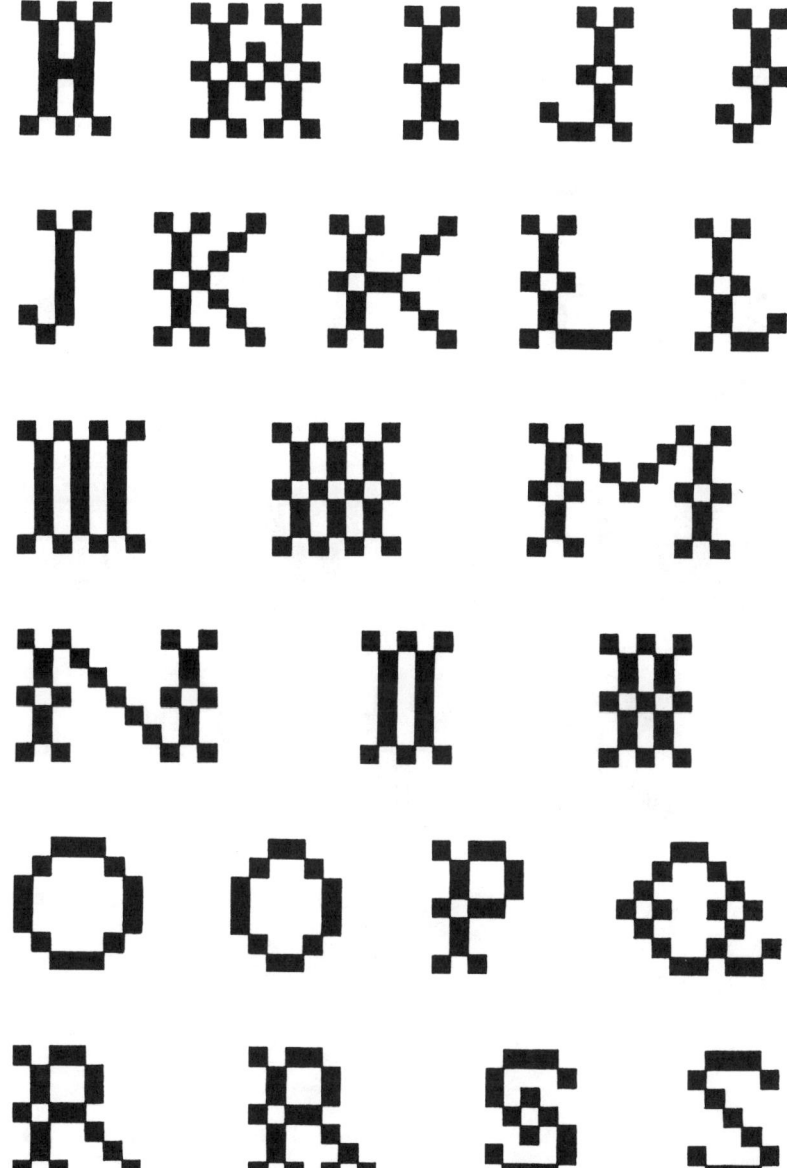

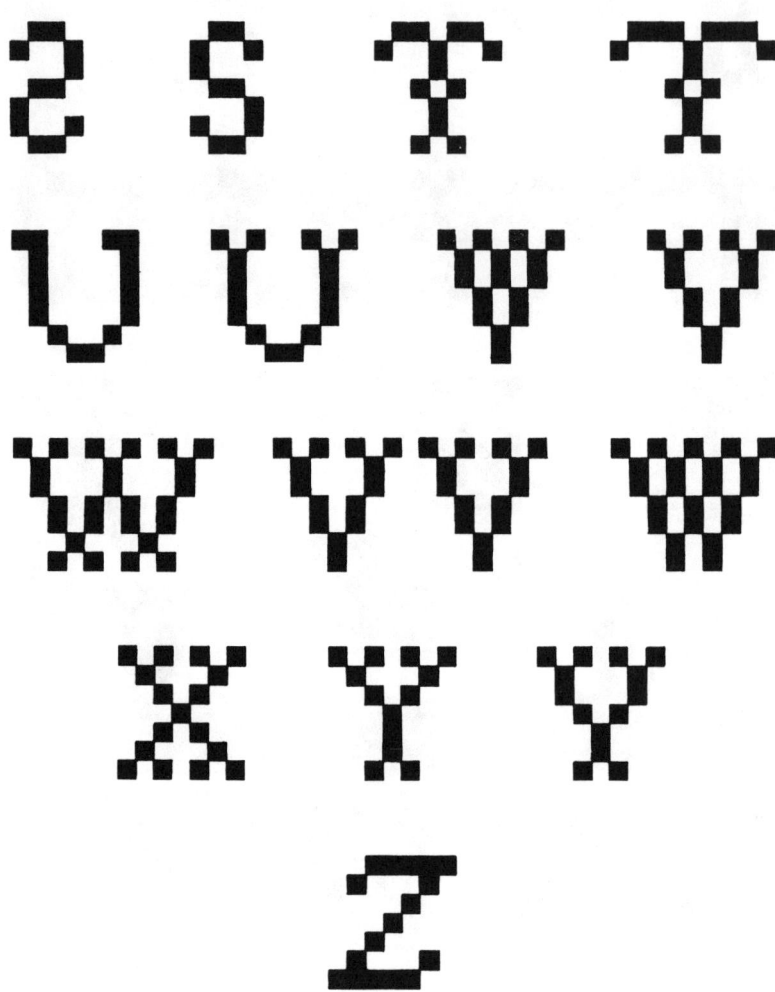

Graphics: Winifred Reddall and Jane Cook

References

1. Catalogue PATCH IN TIME #4, J. Gross and Associates, 1979.
2. Patsy and Myron Orlofsky, QUILTS IN AMERICA, McGraw-Hill, NY 1974, p 216, plate 74.
3. Carleton L. Safford and Robert Bishop, AMERICA'S QUILTS & COVERLETS, E.P. Dutton, NY 1974, p 137.
4. Robert Bishop, NEW DISCOVERIES IN AMERICA QUILTS, E.P. Dutton, NY, 1975, p 32.
5. LADIES CIRCLE PATCHWORK QUILTS, No. 17, 1980, p 22.
6. Orlofsky, p 217.
7. Bishop, p 33.
8. Margaret B. Schiffer, HISTORICAL NEEDLEWORK OF PENNSYLVANIA, CROWN, NY 1968, pp 74, 121.
9. Ethel S. Bolton and Eva J. Coe, AMERICAN SAMPLERS, Dover, NY 1973, pp 109, 132, 150.
10. Bonnie Leman and Judy Martin, LOG CABIN QUILTS, Moon Over the Mountain Publishing Co., Denver 1980, p 35.

Special Presentation

Afro-American Women and Quilts
Introductory Essay
Cuesta Benberry

When I first began my research of "Afro-American Women and Quilts," I did not know anyone else was engaged in a similar investigation. For about twenty years, I had researched and studied quilt history. Occasionally, I acquired information about black quilt makers, which I put in my general information file. During the Bicentennial Year, there was great emphasis on learning about one's ethnic heritage. I thought, why not study Afro-Americans' contributions to quilts as a specific project? I extracted from my general information file all references I had about black quilt makers to form the nucleus of this project. I then began, in earnest, to acquire more data.

Later, I learned that there was intense research being conducted on black women's quilts. I found that there were at least a half-dozen masters' theses or doctoral dissertations being prepared on the subject. In fact, most of the research on black women's quilts was coming from the world of academia - from ethnologists, from anthropologists, folklorists and art historians.

The knowledge of the existence of this other research gave me pause. I wondered about the usefulness of what I was doing. Was I futilely going over plowed ground? I read and studied what was available of the academians' research, before continuing with my own. Why did I decide to continue? It was my perception that there was considerable difference in research from the point of view of the academians, and from my point of view, working as a quilt historian. This was not a qualitative evaluation of the two types of research - an idea that one was superior to

---

Cuesta Benberry, MA, University of Missouri at St. Louis, is a reading specialist in the St. Louis public schools. She has studied quilt patterns since 1960, later general quilt history. Author of many articles on pattern history in **NIMBLE NEEDLE TREASURES, QUILTER'S NEWSLETTER** and **QUILTERS' JOURNAL**. Address: 5150 Terry Ave., St. Louis, MO 63115.

AFRO-AMERICAN WOMEN AND QUILTS

the other. It was simply that the two types are different.

Working as a quilt historian, I am investigating the role of quilts, in an historical context, in the lives of black Americans. This means quilts made by black women, and quilts *not* made by black women, but which have a relationship to their lives. Why did I include quilts made by white women in my "Afro-American Women and Quilts" project? A study of these quilts portray, in a very vivid manner, the concepts of a large segment of white Americans about black Americans, at various points in American history.

For example, in the pre-Civil War slavery days, quilts made by white Americans, such as Slave Chain, or Underground Railroad denote sympathy for the plight of the black slaves. No stronger partisan political statement from this era can be found than the Radical Rose quilt, with its symbolic black center. And to think it came from that second most non-political group of Americans - women!

Next, take a look at the early part of the 20th century. There was increasing industrialization, a movement from rural to urban areas by both blacks and whites, usually to specific and separate living areas, and the rise of black ghettos. The result was increased isolation of the races. Consequently, there were countless white Americans who did not know one black person. There were white people in certain areas who had never seen a black person. So how is this historical period portrayed in quilts of white Americans? Often, they resorted to using the information available to them from the popular communications media of the time — magazines, newspapers, books and the radio. Unfortunately for blacks, during this period, they were seldom presented in any manner except a stereotypical one. Unfortunately, for whites, many believed these stereotypes represented a true picture of blacks. So, from this period, we find quilts with "little wall-eyed pickaninnies," obese Mammies with huge blood-red lips, and lazy "Rastus"-type men. I firmly believe that few women would undertake the huge amount of work involved in quilt making to ridicule anyone. At this point in time, the makers sincerely believed they were constructing quilts which realistically portrayed black people.

What about quilts made by white Americans in the latter part of the 20th century - the present time? Have their concepts of black people changed? Yes, radically. Quilts made today display a great sensitivity to the black experience. There has been a thorough study of African art history resulting in quilts with authentic African designs. There have been quilts made about noted Afro-American historical figures such as Harriet Tubman and Sojourner Truth. From a *quilt historian's* point of view, one is compelled to include quilts made by white Americans about black Americans in order to obtain a full and complete picture of "Afro-American Women and Quilts."

For the most part, the university scholars have concentrated their studies on a specific type of Afro-American quilt. This is a quilt with an African design heritage - an ethnic quilt. These are appliqued quilts, appliqued in the African manner, with motifs that are highly symbolic, rather than realistic. These are also pieced quilts, whose designs reflect African textile construction techniques. They are variously called strippy quilts, string quilts, improvisationally pieced quilts or asymetrically pieced quilts. Contrary to what many people believe, these exuberant, unorthodox, often humorous ethnic quilts by Afro-Americans, are not the work of unskilled quilt makers. I, too, have researched the African design heritage quilt. It is included in my study as part of the picture, but not the whole canvas.

An historical approach requires me to scrutinize *all* types of quilts made by black women, including the Euro-American traditional quilt. The Euro-American traditional quilt, made by black women, is not given much credence by academic researchers. Why? It does appear the academians, more or less, dismiss Euro-American traditional quilts by black women, as *derivative*. All Afro-American quilt making was derivative. The making of bed quilts was a wholly new and learned skill acquired by the Africans in America.

Although there were no bed quilts in sub-Saharan west Africa, the imported west African slave women seemed to have made the transition into the craft of quilt making with relative ease. The slave woman's affinity for quilt making appears to have developed because in her background, she already had a familiarity or the skills necessary for making quilts - applique, piecing and embroidery. So, while the object (the bed quilt) was new to her, the techniques for making it were not.

The strands of the story of "Afro-American Women and Quilts" are many and varied. Some components are:

    the slave-made quilts that represent the black women's earliest attempts at the craft of quilt making;
    the ethnic quilts that demonstrate the tenacity with which the cultural ties with Africa were retained;
    the black-made Euro-American traditional quilts that represent the assimilation of the American culture; the American in Afro-Americans; and
    the historical changes in the perceptions of black Americans by

white Americans, as demonstrated in quilts made by whites, in which blacks are the prime subject matter. And my research of Afro-American quilts goes on.

Special Presentation

White Work Classification System*

Jean Taylor Federico

White work bedcoverings date from the neoclassical period (1790-1830) of American decorative arts. The beauty of all white work resulted from an infinite number of intricate stitches which produced dramatic three dimensional qualities. Most of these bedcoverings feature a large central motif; the designs were suited to the revival and reinterpretation of Greco-Roman motifs inspired by the finds at Herculaneum and Pompeii. The white surface area of bedcoverings during this period is yet another interpretation of "classical purity." The same florals, cornucopias, wreaths, urns, medallions, and tassels will be found on textiles as well as furniture, glass and ceramics of the period.

There are three major types of white work bedcovering: embroidery, candlewicking, and Marseilles quilting or stuffed work. The latter two classifications are further divided depending upon whether the example is hand or machine worked. Often two or more of these techniques could be combined. It is especially common to find candlewicking combined with embroidery. One often finds examples of stuffed work (or Marseilles quilting) combined with either applique or piece work in in the early 19th century.

White embroidery on a white linen or cotton ground provided an effective decorative technique for bedcoverings. These embroidered bedspreads should not be confused with candlewick spreads because they employ flat embroidery techniques which do not rely on the French knot to achieve a nubby effect. Often these spreads feature the names, birth or wedding dates, and residences of their makers or recipients. The

---

Jean Taylor Federico, MA, University of Michigan, is Curator of the D.A.R. Museum in Washington, DC. She has studied and taught widely in American Decorative Arts and has many publications on decorative arts and folk artists. Address: The D.A.R. Museum, 1776 D Street NW, Washington, DC 20006.

*Copyright QUILTERS' JOURNAL. Used with permission. All examples cited are in the collection of the D.A.R. Museum.

embroidery yarn is cotton, sometimes two ply cotton, and the flowers and vines have become more open and more swirled. An embroidered bedspread of about 1815 shows a variety of stitches, but they all produce a flat outline and texture. This particular bedspread was made in Laurens County, South Carolina.

Of the dozen embroidered bedspreads which have family histories in the DAR collection, they are predominately from Virginia, South Carolina and Kentucky. None of them is from the North, nor is any of metropolitan origin. Exclusively they seem to be southern and rural. As such they show less of the neoclassical inspiration in their decoration, tending to be more naturalistic. Very often these flower-vine decorations have been called The Tree of Life motif. It would probably be more appropriate to assume that the decorations were more closely associated with crewelwork or with the popular designs of printed chintz from the end of the 18th century. Also, since these bedcoverings tend to be southern and rural, it is quite possible that some of these wool yarns were not available or alternatively that the desire for certain kinds of patterns existed longer in a more rural area.

Candlewick refers to the soft bulky yarn used as an embroidery material. Candlewick spreads could be made by machine or by hand. Usually handmade candlewick spreads are limited to the use of French knots. Sometimes the knots are not the classic French knot done in silk embroidery, but because the yarn is particularly nubby, a knot-like effect is achieved. Actually these stitches are much more like the basic outline stitch in embroidery. Many women, however, achieved different effects with other stitches, and by clipping the exposed wick or threads. This is often called tufting, and when the candlewicks were close together, it produced a sculpturally interesting effect. Machine-made candlewick bed-spreads continue to be popular today and are usually referred to by their manufacturer as "heirloom" or erroneously as "colonial style."

An exceptionally fine machine-made candlewick was made in Philadelphia in 1834 and carries the name "William H. and Mary Fowler." A large star forms the center with small stars and flowers along the border. The designs, when executed by machine, appear geometric in form. A flower border shows the linear quality which is characteristic of the machine-made spreads. These machine-made examples are woven in one panel and are not seamed.

In contrast, the handmade candlewick bedspread of Alida Holmes of Montgomery Co., N.Y. 1812 is executed in French knots. It features a central panel with the federal eagle and "E Pluribus Unum." The two borders surrounding the central panel show neoclassical tassels and swags. Another handmade candlewick bedspread made by Lydia Barker in 1827 is executed on a huckaback weave cotton. The central panel contrasts again with the distinctive linear or geometric quality of the Fowler machine-made example. In addition, the reverse side of the handmade candlewicked spread shows a plethora of knots and yarn. The machine-made examples are completely plain. The handmade Barker bedspread is constructed of 3 panels, each approximately 29" in width. Ribbed cotton is another commonly seen type of weave on candlewick bedspreads. There are also combinations of embroidery and candlewicking.

A great deal has been written about the very popular stuffed work of this period, usually employing the name "trapunto", which is in fact a 20th century term for an 18th century style of needlework. Advertisements appeared throughout the 18th century in America for two types of Marseilles quilting: the entirely handmade work which resembles these stuffed or corded bed-coverings or the "loom quilting or Mock quilting" which was machine-made and imported to America (Susan Swan PLAIN AND FANCY, New York 1977: pg. 229). The 19th century examples of this work were often referred to as Marseilles quilting. One of the machine-made examples in our collection, which was received in 1943 with a reliable family history of use in the mid-19th century, was called a "Marseilles spread." Unfortunately 'trapunto' has been used so frequently to describe these bedcoverings that we have tended to forget the proper 18th and 19th century terms.

Women had often employed the technique of Marseilles quilting during the 18th century — but for their petticoats. Until the end of the 18th century the construction of dresses left a front panel exposed from the waist to the hem. Many of the petticoats were quilted (not just for warmth), but because the technique was particularly attractive, especially on the solid color garments which were often coordinated with the color of the dress. The 19th century use of Marseilles quilting is an outgrowth of this 18th century popular form which was not only useful, but highly decorative.

Marseilles quilting was not really quilting, which implies the use of a batting or third layer of fabric between the two outer layers. Instead, there are only two layers of fabric and cord or cotton on the inside. A loosely woven fabric was selected for the backing, so that the yarn, cord or cotton could be stuffed or drawn through from the back. The top layer was more finely woven fabric. The maker outlined her design with very fine stitches, stitching the two layers together at the same time.

WHITE WORK CLASSIFICATION

Then she used a bodkin, a blunt-eyed needle shaped instrument or a large-eyed needle to force the yarn, thread or cotton between the stitched-down area.

Despite the number of intricate stitches required to do Marseilles quilting, women continued making these attractive bedcoverings until the 1830's. However, machines soon replaced the hands and Marseilles spreads became popular. The fabric used in the machine-made examples is completely different in texture and appearance from the handmade Marseilles quilting examples. Both sides are relatively loosely woven with horizontal rows of thick cording between. By comparison, the stuffed areas are nearly flat. What had been the running stitch or rows of diagonal stitches on the handmade variety, now appears to look like rows of small pin holes. The pattern is formed from the lack of this machine stitch in certain planned areas which are deliberately left blank. Thus, there is really no stuffing at all. These spreads are usually not seamed, and one example is approximately 105" square.

This classification system should be useful and effective for early 19th century white work. The use of consistent, proper terminology for these examples will aid in classifying these works. It is especially important that we attempt to drop from our vocabularies the term 'trapunto' which was never used in the early 19th century. While Marseilles quilts appear often on early 19th century inventories, I have never seen the term 'trapunto'. Stuffed work executed today should be called just that, "stuffed work."

Special Presentation

Archiving and the American Quilt:
A Position Paper

John L. Oldani

For decades, the oral tradition, representing everything from the spoken word through the gesture and folk handicraft, had been curiously neglected by scholars as unworthy of serious consideration because of the frivolous nature of the study or the lack of relations to the human condition. Folklore, it was often held, was nothing more than "old stories" or superstitions, or even, "dirty jokes." In comparatively recent times, the recognition of the importance of studying the lore of a group, through extensive fieldwork, and within context, has become academically important and even, ashamedly, "in." Symbolistically, it is held that the oral traditions, as means of transmitting culture, reveal much of a person and his culture; absurdly, it is believed that such a study is a clear way to "collect jokes" without working. The latter point of view has led to much that is gross in the field; the former, if understood properly, gives strong merit to the study as worthy culture reflection.

The folk art or folk handicraft that is quilting represents a microcosm of this briefly described academic problem within folklore. But, different from the whole world of folklore, quilting has some special considerations, which are not often made or understood, and the products of its analysis are very often ephemeral, vulgar, and certainly gross. To be sure, quilting may be ideal folklore in its learned methodology, its anonymous authorship of patterns, its different versions for techniques and naming, and the traditional and formalized way it is internalized. Yet, quilting, because of its purpose, its appeal, its

---

John L. Oldani, Ph.D., St. Louis University, is Associate Professor of American Studies in the Department of English, and Director of the Folklore Archives at Southern Illinois University at Edwardsville. He coordinated the quilt show at the Museum of Westward Expansion in 1980. Address: Box 43, SIUE, Edwardsville, IL 62025.

beauty, has often fallen into the hands of would-be folklorists/scholars who, daily, produce the "definitive" work on the subject. A real phenomenon in interest in quilts has become a national mania and frenzy. Most often, capitalism has intruded, and the resultant stories, in themselves, become a part of urban folklore, if not part of supernatural legends!

This unfortunate effect has little direction, little purpose and little leadership. What is needed are clear methodology, proper training in the field, archiving techniques, the perception of the quilt in context, a real understanding of the "maker" in relation to the handmade object, and an analysis of the collection as historically and sociologically important. It is in this connection with folklore that quilting can be seen as a direct microcosm of the problems of acceptance which the field of folklore as had. But just as folklore has achieved some direction and added immensely to the study of people, so, too, quilting, if studied properly, can produce effective results as part of the study of folk art and handicrafts while reflecting on the artist within context.

In the following discussion, it will be shown how one approach has been taken as a solution to the problem, the purposes of this approach, the larger perspective involved in the study, and possible indeces for the future study of the quilt. By such a discussion, it is hoped that at least one part of a folklife study can be steered properly into a directed study, worthy of research before it becomes a "needle hysteria."

In 1974, the Folklore Archive at Southern Illinois University at Edwardsville began the first Quilt Archive in the United States, which was devoted entirely to the study of the quilt in America and based in an academic setting. The purposes for such an undertaking are many and varied. Basically, the quilt, historically and folkloristically, is the ideal handicraft. Moreover, the American woman, almost exclusively, made and designed quilts as part of her unrecognized genius. Also, the study and collection had never been done formally and an established Archive would be a perfect place in which to house, catalogue, cross-index, and verify much of the classifications which are in quilting. What the Archive does, simply, is celebrate an American folk art!

Initially, since the Archive operates without a budget, letters were sent to several informants in southern Illinois, known for their quilting and previously identified on other fieldwork trips. These letters outlined the plans for the Archive and the purpose for collecting things related to quilting. The idea grew with no publicity, but with the crusading spirit of a few quilting women who deeply believed in their work and purposes for doing it. Soon, actual quilt blocks were sent to the Archive from all parts of the U.S. Each was made from a pattern familiar to or loved by the quilter, with no specifications as to size or quilting, since there was no wish to stifle creativity, the life spirit of folklore. Each was catalogued as to the name of the block, which represents folk naming and folk vocabulary, the quilter who made it, which represents the quilt in context, and the city and state where the quilter lives, which repesents comparative folklore. If for instance, a block from one part of the country is identical to a block from another part, but each has a different name, the example becomes doubly important.

With many of the submissions of blocks there was information about the quilting technique itself. The maker often mentioned her techniques, where she learned to quilt, in what atmosphere she quilted, what quilting "does" for her, the why of her obsession, her traditional approach today, and often her reaction to another form of quilting. Many times, the informant would be pursued for additional information to be included in the larger Archive. All of the information was placed in an informant file which was easily cross-indexed for other purposes, such as ethnicity or rural vs. urban lore.

Patterns for quilts are gradually added to the Archive so that it can serve as an ideal depository for those wishing to perpetuate the art of quilting and needing a pattern which they formerly had, but had misplaced, or had seen somewhere else. Historically, the patterns themselves are important in their reflection of the times in which they were conceived. Often some historical event catalyzed the mind of the woman, like Clay's Choice, or Watergate, or Cleveland's Favorite, or Whig Rose. Often, too, newspapers printed patterns for quilts in their weekly editions. Such patterns were often devised by women with homey pseudonyms; some were variations on popular patterns; but all kept the tradition of quilting alive. The Nancy Cabot and Kansas City Star patterns, as examples of the latter, are important as primary sources for the Archive to have. Again, they are often used as comparative folklore if in nothing more than comparing the different approaches to quilting, then and now.

The Archive has also collected slides of quilts from all parts of the country. Since a full-sized quilt is valuable, with special needs for storing, and therefore almost impossible to place, the slides serve as concrete representations of the variety in quilting. More importantly, they can be used by scholars in the field more easily, handily, and efficiently, to compare, to observe stitches per inch, to compare setting, and even to understand color sense and textile formula.

The quilt can also contribute much to the traditional folk celebration and the study thereof by exhibitions, workshops, and symposia. To this end, the Archive, annually, since 1977, has produced a quilt show, non-juried, to emphasize the importance of the collection, the quilts, and the need for a proper recognition in the study of them. At the most recent show, more than 400 quilts, from all parts of the U.S were displayed — a certain testimony to the popularity and renaissance of the art form.

Recently, the Archive has begun applying the quilt art form to the quilter as contextual. In which settings did the quilt itself begin to form? Where did the quilter learn her skills? Whom does she teach? Why are her patterns selected as they are? What is discussed at her quilting parties? Why the quilting club? It is the strong belief of the Archive that the folk object cannot be known apart from its maker. By analyzing the interviews, this approach can be utilized. Furthermore, much folklore can be added to the larger Archive in the vocabularly, superstitions, legends and jokes collected as part of the whole area of quilting. To be sure, the latter exists within the whole world of folklife. And, also, the place of the woman in American folklore is often clearer through an analysis of her exclusive art.

As an example of some of the holdings, the following is a partial list of quilt patterns which the Archive holds in trust:
Jane Alan Patterns
American Needlework Patterns
Aunt Kate's Quilt Bee, 1964-1977
Aunt Martha's Quilt Books
Aunt Martha's Quilt Patterns (through 9,998)
Nancy Cabot Books, 1 through 50
Nancy Cabot Quilt Patterns, A-Z
Country Gentlewoman (through 11212)
Mrs. Danner's Quilt Patterns (A-Z)
Detroit News Quilt Patterns
Farm Journal Quilt Patterns
Betty Flack Quilt Patterns
Glover Quilt Patterns
Halls Quilt Patterns
Hearth and Home Quilt Patterns
Ruby Hinson Quilt Patterns
Home Arts Quilt Patterns
Kansas City Star Quilt Patterns
Ladies Art Company, Quilt Patterns
McKim Quilt Patterns

Marvel Art Company, Quilt Patterns
Mountain Mist, Quilt Patterns
Paragon Quilt Patterns
Progressive Farmer Patterns
Rainbow Block Company
Stearns and Foster Company, Quilt Patterns
Laura Wheeler Quilt Patterns through 7500
Workbasket Quilts

The above are available to interested laymen and scholars who are researching in the area, whether it be textiles, folk naming, or the quilt itself.

The Quilt Archive at Southern Illinois University at Edwardsville is a concrete attempt to institutionalize the quilt. It collects and classifies patterns by name, type and age; it documents quilt blocks by name, maker, city and state; it cross-indexes materials related to the maker of the quilt: the materials of her craft; it presents slides as documents for comparative folklore. Sociologically, the Archive speaks to the American woman's place in folklore and folklife. Contextually, it places disparate elements of a folklore in a centralized depository, subtracting that which is popular and vulgar, and adding that which is a vital part of a folk tradition. In this real, humble beginning, it is congruent with the purposes of the study of folklore itself, and it freezes a classification before it is lost forever.

The American Quilt Study Group is a nonprofit organization devoted to uncovering and disseminating the history of quiltmaking as a significant part of American art and culture. AQSG encourages and supports research on quilts, quiltmaking, quiltmakers, and the textiles and materials of quilts. Membership and participation are open to all interested persons. For further information, contact the American Quilt Study Group, 660 Mission Street, Suite 400, San Francisco, CA 94105.

American Quilt Study Group Publications List

Uncoverings 1980 (Vol. 1) (ISBN 0-9606590-0-5).
Contents: Benberry, *Afro-American Women and Quilts*; Brackman, *Midwestern Pattern Sources*; Federico, *White Work*; Garoutte, *Quilts in a Bedding Context*; Gross, *20th Century Quiltmakers*; Hilty, *Passion for Quiltmaking*; Metzler-Smith, *A Pomo Indian Quilt*; Oldani, *S.I.U.E. Quilt Archives*; Ramsey, *Country Quilt Design Invention*; Reddall, *Lettered Quilts*.
(76 pages, 9 illustrations)

Uncoverings 1981 (Vol. 2) (ISBN 0-9606590-1-3).
Contents: Bonfield, *19th Century Cloth, Clothing and Quilts*; Brackman, *Quilts at Chicago Fairs*; Cozart, *Quilts in American Literature*; Davis, *Contemporary Quilters*; De Graw, *Museum Collecting*; Garoutte, *California's First Quilting*; Glover, *An Alabama Quilt Collection*; Jarrell, *Three Historic Quilts*; Koob, *Documenting Quilts by Fabrics*; Mathieson, *Mariner's Compass*.
(112 pages, 20 illustrations, index)

Uncoverings 1982 (Vol. 3) (ISBN 0-9606590-2-1).
Contents: Brackman, *Hall/Szabronski Collection*; Brown, *Cuna Molas*; Cross, *Wood's Family Quilts*; Eanes, *Nine Quilts of Mecklenburg County*; Garoutte, *Marseilles Quilts and Woven Offspring*; Hersh, *1809 Quilting Designs*; de Julio, *Betsey Reynolds Voorhees Collection*; Malanyn, *Fifteen Dearborn Quilts*; Nickols, *String Quilts*; Rowley, *Red Cross Quilts*.
(140 pages, 43 illustrations, index)

Uncoverings 1983 (Vol. 4) (ISBN 0-9606590-3-X).
Contents: Benberry, *White Perspectives of Blacks*; Brackman, *Index to Pieced Patterns*; Caudle, *Maine Quiltmakers*; Christopherson, *Documenting Quilts*; Church, *Stenciled Quilts*; Gunn, *Template Patchwork Patterns*; Horton, *Macon County Quilts*; Ramsey, *Childhood Memories Quilt*; Reichelt-Jordan, *Patchwork Around the World*; Yabsley, *Button Blankets on the Northwest Coast*. (152 pages, 39 illustrations, index)

Uncoverings 1984 (Vol. 5) (ISBN 0-9606590-4-8).

Contents: Burdick, *Talula Bottoms' Quilts*; Cozart, *Fundraising Quilts: 1860-1960*; Gunn, *Crazy Quilts and Outline Quilts*; Hersh, *18th Century Quilted Petticoats*; Horton, *South Carolina's Quilts*; Liles, *Dyes in American Quilts*; Meyer, *Missouri-German Quilts*; Todaro, *A Family of Texas Quilters*; Townsend, *Kansas City Star Quilt Patterns*; Waldvogel, *WPA Milwaukee Quilts*.
(170 pages, 41 illustrations, index)

Uncoverings 1985 (Vol. 6) (ISBN 0-9606590-5-6).

Contents: Allen, *Kent County Bed Coverings 1710-1820*; Boynton, *Changes in Amish Quilting*; Garoutte, *Early Textiles in Hawaii*; Gunn, *Northern Civil War Quilts*; Havig, *Missouri Quilts*; Horton, *Civil War Quilts in South Carolina*; Joseph, *Quilt and Batik Production*; Kirkpatrick, *Quilts and the Progressive Farmer*; Lasansky, *Pennsylvania Haps*; Schilmoeller, *Children's Literature*.
(170 pages, 30 illustrations, index)

Uncoverings 1986 (Vol. 7) (ISBN 0-9606590-6-4).

Contents: Benberry, *Quilt Cottage Industries*; Cozart, *An Early 19th Century Quiltmaker*; Cunningham, *Fourteen Quilts*; Davis, *Quilts and Quilters of Floyd County Virginia*; Hersh, *Primitive Hall Quilt Top*; Kirkpatrick, *Uncle Eli's Quilting Party*; Nicoll, *Delaware Valley Quaker Signature Quilts, 1840-1860*; Pickens, *Scrap Quilts of New Mexico*; Ramsey, *Floral Designs in Southern Quiltmaking*; Smith, *Quilt Blocks? or Quilt "Patterns"?*
(150 pages, 27 illustrations, index)

Uncoverings 1987 (Vol. 8) (ISBN 0-9606590-8-0).

Contents: Gero, *Australian Patriotic Quilts*; Gunn, *Yo-Yo or Bed of Roses Quilts*; Hall-Patton, *Southern California Quiltmakers*; Henley, *Alabama Gunboat Quilts*; Horton, *Frank C. Brown Collection*; Murphy, *An Unnamed Regional Pattern*; Przybysz, *Great American Quilt Festival*; Roberson, *North Carolina Quilt Project*; Waldvogel, *Southern Linsey Quilts*; Gunn, Brackman, Horton and Smith, Presentation: *How I Do Research*.
(176 pages, 30 illustrations, index)

Uncoverings 1988 (Vol. 9) (ISBN 0-9606590-7-2).
Contents: Bonfield, *Diaries of New England Quilters*; Gunn, *Quilts at Ohio Fairs*; Horton, *Textile Industry and South Carolina Quilts*; Kirkpatrick, *Alamance Plaids*; Long, *Quiltmaking in the Church of the Brethren*; Nickols, *Cotton Sacks in Quiltmaking*; Peaden, *Donated Quilts Warmed Wartorn Europe*; Ramsey, *Quiltmaking by African-American Women*; Rolfe, *Quilting: Its Absence in Australia*; Stonuey and Crews, *Nebraska Quilt History Project*. (204 pages, 40 illustrations, index)

Uncoverings 1989 (Vol. 10) (ISBN 1-877859-00-1).
Contents: Ballard, *Ladies Aid of Hope Lutheran Church*; Brackman, *Signature Quilts*; Burdick, *Julia Boyer Reinstein Collection*; Gunn, *Quilts for Milady's Boudoir*; Meyer, *Early Influences of the Sewing Machine*; Przybysz, *Contemporary Quilted Garments*; Shea and Crews, *Nebraska Quiltmakers: 1870-1940*; Sienkiewicz, *The Marketing of Mary Evans*; Trechsel, *Mourning Quilts*; Ramsey, Presentation: *Tribute to Mariska Karasz*.
(166 pages, 23 illustrations, index)

Uncoverings 1990 (Vol. 11) (ISBN 1-877859-01-X).
Contents: Carruth and Sinema, *Emma Andres and Her Six Grand Old Characters*; Langellier, *Contemporary Quiltmaking in Maine*; Peaden, *Multicolored Geometric Pieced Sails of Mindanao*; Phillippi, *Quilt Tops in New York* ; Richards, Martin-Scott and Maguire, *Quilts as Material History*; Smith, *Quilt History in Old Periodicals*; Stehlik, *Omaha World-Herald Quilt Patterns*; Tuckhorn, *Quilts at the DAR Museum*; Waldvogel, *Anne Orr's Quilts*;
(216 pages, 40 illustrations, index)

Uncoverings 1991 (Vol. 12) (ISBN1-877-859-02-8).
Contents: Cerny, *A Quilt Guild and Female Identity*; Ciani, *Machado Quilt*; Howe, *NAMES Project*; Kendra, *Economics of Contemporary Appalachian Quilting*; Mahan, *Quilts in Old Photographs*; Nickols, *Mary A. McElwain*; Riffe, *Brain Dominance and Quilters*; Williams, *Tradition and Art: Two Layers of Meaning*; Wilson, *Quiltmaking in Counties Antrim and Down*;
(218 pages, 32 illustrations, index)

Technical Guides

#1 Tracing the Quiltmaker by Patricia Mooney Melvin
Explores examination of public records and organizational documents in order to glean information on quiltmakers as individuals.

#2 The Oral Interview in Quilt Research by Laurel Horton
Explains how oral testimony plays a major role in gathering information which may not be available in written or printed sources.

#3 The Care and Conservation of Quilts by Virginia Gunn
Current thinking about safe ways to display, use, store, clean, and repair quilts with emphasis on methods appropriate for individuals in homes and small historical agencies.

#4 Dating Antique Quilts by Barbara Brackman
Two hundred years of style, pattern, and technique; the basics of comparative dating.

#5 Quilt Documentation: Planning a Quilt Day
by Jeannette Lasansky
Details the practical aspects of holding quilt days and conducting regional quilt conferences.

For a current price list, please contact:

American Quilt Study Group
660 Mission St., Suite 400
San Francisco, CA 94105

phone: 415 495-0163
FAX: 415 495-3516

AQSG
- sponsors an exciting seminar each year
- publishes an annual volume, *Uncoverings*
- maintains a library and research facility
- produces a series of *Technical Guides*
- publishes the newsletter, *Blanket Statements*
- offers research grants and scholarships
- serves as an information center

AMERICAN QUILT STUDY GROUP

AQSG's goal is to develop a responsible and accurate body of information about quilts and their makers. A reliable history of quiltmaking provides insights into the lives and times of quiltmakers, and connects women with their heritage and their place in creative art.

We welcome all persons interested in the history of quiltmaking. Our members include quilt lovers, traditional and contemporary quilt artists, dealers, collectors, researchers, authors, museum curators, students of women's studies, and folklorists.

Discover the thrill of dating your grandmother's quilt from its fabrics, or of tracing the great quilt you bought at a flea market back to its maker.

Membership in AQSG opens the door to a wonderful network of people who are passionate about quilts and whose interests range across every level of quilting.

The American Quilt Study Group is dedicated to preserving the story of quiltmaking – past, present, and future. We invite you to join our ranks!

"No other group has done as much as AQSG to document and preserve America's quilt history. If you only support one quilt organization, this is the one!"
—Julie Silber, Quilt Curator, Lecturer

"The American Quilt Study Group has maintained its commitment to sound and significant quilt scholarship. Its annual journal, Uncoverings, *is a must for those seriously interested in the subject."*
—Jonathan Holstein, Quilt Historian, Author

YES! I would like to join AQSG, and help preserve our quilting heritage for generations to follow.

[ ]$35 Friend   [ ]$100 Associate   [ ]$250 Benefactor
[ ]$500 Sponsor   [ ]$1000 Patron   [ ]$100 GUILD

Foreign Memberships: Canadians add $1.50, all other countries add $15 for extra postage. U.S. funds only.

NAME_____

ADDRESS_____

CITY/STATE/ZIP_____

PHONE ( )_____

My check for $_____ payable to AQSG is enclosed.

Mail to: AQSG, 660 Mission Street, Suite 300   Tel: (415) 495-0163
San Francisco, CA 94105-4001   Fax: (415) 495-3516